Simplified RECIPES for DAY CARE CENTERS

PATRICIA D. ASMUSSEN, R. D.

Jule Wilkinson, Editor

Published by Cahners Books
A Division of Cahners Publishing Company, Inc.
89 Franklin Street, Boston, Mass. 02110
Publishers of Institutions/Volume Feeding Magazine

ISBN 0-8436-0590-1

Library of Congress Catalog Card No. 74-222

Printed in the United States of America

Contents

To my mother who spent many hours during my early childhood years making nutritious oatmeal and raisin cookies; and during my adolescent years had the patience to let me learn to cook; and in my college years provided the financial and emotional encouragement for me to become a dietitian.

Preface

It is a pleasure to introduce this book for use as a guide in the preparation of food for Day-Care Centers. An essential part and responsibility of Day-Care Centers is to provide food for children in adequate quantity and quality to meet nutritional needs. The preparation of food which is palatable, attractive, nutritional and safe is the goal of those working in these food services.

This first edition of Simplified Recipes for Day-Care Centers is designed to aid those preparing food for children from 2 to 6 years in age. It is hoped that the cooks will find it a valuable resource tool to improve the nutritional care of the children for whom they serve.

Arlene Wilson, R. D.
Associate Director of Department
of Nutrition and Dietetics
Director of Dietetic Internship
Indiana University–Purdue University
at Indianapolis–Medical Center Campus

Introduction

THIS RECIPE BOOK has been designed for you, the day care center cook, as a tool to help you in planning, preparing, and serving meals and snacks to our tomorrow–the young children of today.

The recipes are based on 25 child-size servings to meet the nutritional needs and appetites of the average child two to six years of age. Amounts are given in standard measures since most centers' kitchens are equipped to measure instead of weighing ingredients. You will note that if the ingredient is a canned item, the number and size of retail containers are listed since many centers are not large enough to use institutional size containers or No. 10 cans efficiently. For the larger centers, please note under the General Information Section a conversion chart for retail size containers and institutional size containers.

It is hard to standardize pan sizes as they vary from center to center. The recipes have pan sizes listed, if you do not have that particular size pan, experiment with the pans you do have and make a note on the recipe as to the pan or pans you find suitable for preparing the recipe in your particular kitchen.

Use this recipe book as a workbook. The two blank portion columns are for you to complete in order to individualize the recipe to meet your requirements, whether you serve 25, 50, or 200 children. At the back of each section you will find blank recipe forms; these are for the addition of your favorite recipes and for new recipes you discover or develop in your career.

You may miss many items considered standard for a recipe book. Recipes are not included if the package the item comes in universally contains the directions for preparation. (Example: rice, pastas, instant potatoes, mixes, etc.) Since there is a wide variety of quality mixes and convenience items available, not too many baked items from "scratch" have been included knowing your time is also limited. The book is a sampling of recipes and ideas which I hope will help you in your very important job.

Developing good eating habits begins in early childhood and is the foundation of nutrition education. A variety of foods, well prepared and attractively served to children in a happy and loving atmosphere result in the attitude "food is good–food is fun."

General Information

LADLE SIZES

1/4 cup (2 ounces)
1/2 cup (4 ounces)
3/4 cup (6 ounces)
1 cup (8 ounces)

SCOOP SIZES

Scoop Number	Level Measure
6	2/3 cup
8	1/2 cup
10	2/5 cup
12	1/3 cup
16	1/4 cup
20	3-1/5 tablespoons
24	2-2/3 tablespoons
30	2-1/5 tablespoons
40	1-3/5 tablespoons

EQUIVALENTS

16 ounces	1 pound	3 teaspoons	1 tablespoon
8 fluid ounces	1 cup	16 tablespoons	1 cup
32 fluid ounces	1 quart	4 cups	1 quart
		4 quarts	1 gallon

A.P. DENOTES "AS PURCHASED"

Apples	1 pound	3 to 4 medium
Apricots, dried A.P.	1 pound	3 cups stewed
Baking Powder	1 ounce	7-1/2 teaspoons
	6-1/2 ounces	1 cup
Bananas, A.P.	1 pound	3 medium
thinly sliced	6 ounces	1 cup (1-1/2 medium)
Blueberries, fresh or frozen	1 pound	3 cups (about)
Cabbage, shredded	8 ounces	1 quart
finely chopped	12 ounces	1 quart
Carrots, shredded	1 pound	1 quart
diced (1/4 inch)	1 pound	3-1/2 cups
Celery, unbleached diced (1/4 inch)	1 pound	3-1/2 cups
Cheese, American, grated	1 pound	1 quart (about)
Cheese, cottage	1 pound	2 cups
Cheese, cream	1 pound	2 cups
Chicken, A.P.	5-6 pounds	1-1/4 pounds, (cooked and boned)
Chocolate	1 pound	1-3/4 cups (melted)
	1 ounce	1 square
Cinnamon, ground	1 ounce	4 tablespoons
Cloves, ground	1 ounce	4 tablespoons
Cocoa	1 pound	4-1/2 cups
Coconut	1 pound	6-7 cups
Coffee, ground	1 pound	5 to 5-1/2 cups
instant	1 ounce	1/2 cup
Corn Meal	1 pound	3 cups
Cornstarch	1 ounce	3-1/3 table-spoons
Cranberries, fresh	1 pound	1 quart
Cucumber, diced	1 pound	3 cups
Dates	1 pound	2-1/2 cups

WEIGHT AND VOLUME OF "AS PURCHASED" COMMONLY USED FOODS

EQUIVALENTS *(cont.)*

Food	Weight	Volume
Eggs (graded large):		
Whole eggs	1 pound	2 cups (10 eggs)
Egg whites	8 ounces	1 cup (8 whites)
Egg yolk	8 ounces	1 cup (12 yolks)
Hard cooked	1 dozen	1 quart, chopped
Eggs, powdered whole	4 ounces	1 cup
Flour		
All-purpose, unsifted	1 pound	3-3/4 cups
Cake flour, sifted	1 pound	4-1/2 cups
Whole wheat	1 pound	3-3/4 cups
Gelatin:		
Plain	1 pound	3 cups
	1 ounce	3 tablespoons
All flavors	1 pound	2-1/3 cups
	7 ounces	1 cup
Grapefruit (size 54)	1 fruit	10-12 sections
	4 fruits	1 quart sections
Ham (cooked)	1 pound	1 quart, chopped
Honey	12 ounces	1 cup
Horse-radish	1 ounce	2 tablespoons
Instant Breakfast	1 pound	2 cups
Lemons:		
Juice (size 360)	12 lemons	2 cups
Rind, grated	1 ounce	1/4 cup
Limes:		
Juice (size 72)	10-12 limes	1 cup
Macaroni, A.P.	1 pound	2-1/2 quarts, cooked
Marshmallows	1 ounce	4 marshmallows
Mayonnaise	1 pound	2 cups (about)
Milk:		
Evaporated (1 can)	14-1/2 ounces	1-5/8 cups
Nonfat dry milk	4 ounces	1 cup
Mint, 1 bunch, A.P.	4 ounces	2 cups, chopped
Molasses	12 ounces	1 cup
Mushrooms, fresh, A.P.	1 pound	1-1/4 quarts, sliced
Mustard, ground	1 ounce	4-2/3 tablespoons
Noodles, medium, A.P.	1 pound	2-1/2 quarts, cooked
Nuts	4 ounces	1 cup, chopped
Nutmeg, ground	1 ounce	3-2/3 tablespoons
Olives, stuffed	6 ounces	1 cup, chopped

chopped	4 ounces	1 cup
finely chopped	6 ounces	1 cup
Oranges:		
Juice (size 216 Florida)	10-12 oranges	1 quart
Rind, grated	1 ounce	1/4 cup
Sections (size 176 California)	12-14 oranges	1 quart
Parsley, chopped	1 ounce	1/4 cup (med. pack)
Peaches:		
Fresh, A.P.	1 pound	2 cups, sliced
Pears, canned	1 pound	8 to 9 halves
	1 pound	2-1/4 cups, diced
Pepper, ground	1 ounce	4 tablespoons
Peppers, green, chopped	5 ounces	1 cup
Pimientos, chopped	8 ounces	1 cup
Pineapple:		
Canned, crushed, drained	6 ounces	1 cup
Canned, crushed with juice	9 ounces	1 cup
Potatoes, cooked and peeled	1 pound	2-3/4 cups, diced
Instant Mashed, (gran)	1 pound	2 cups
(prepared)		
Dehydrated (sliced)	1 pound	2-1/4 quarts
Dehydrated (cooked)	1 pound	2-3/4 cups
Prunes, dried, A.P.	1 pound	3 cups, stewed and drained
Pie Fillings & Puddings:		
Butterscotch	1 pound	2-2/3 cups
Chiffon Pie Fill	1 pound	2-1/4 cups
Chocolate	1 pound	2-2/3 cups
Coconut Cream	1 pound	3 cups (about)
Inst. Butterscotch	1 pound	3 cups
Inst. Chocolate	1 pound	2-7/8 cups
Inst. Vanilla	1 pound	3-1/3 cups
Lemon Pie Filling	1 pound	2-1/8 cups
Vanilla	1 pound	2-1/3 cups
Vanilla Tapioca	1 pound	2-1/2 cups
Raisins, seedless	1 pound	3 cups
Rhubarb, A.P.	1 pound	1 quart, diced
Rice, A.P.	1 pound	2 quarts, cooked
Salmon	1 pound	2 cups, flaked
Salt	1 ounce	2 tablespoons
Shortening:		
Butter or margarine	1 pound	2 cups

WEIGHT AND VOLUME OF "AS PURCHASED" COMMONLY USED FOODS

EQUIVALENTS *(cont.)*

Food	Weight	Volume
Hydrogenated veg. short.	1 pound	2-1/4 cups
Soda, baking	1 ounce	2 tablespoons
Spaghetti, A.P.	1 pound	2-1/4 quarts. cooked
Strawberries:		
Fresh, A.P.	1 quart	2 cups, crushed
	1 quart	3 cups, sliced
Sugar:		
Brown sugar	6 ounces	1 cup, packed
Confectioners' Sugar	4 ounces	1 cup
Granulated sugar	7 ounces	1 cup
Syrups:		
Corn syrup	12 ounces	1 cup
Tapioca	1 pound	3 cups
	1 ounce	3 tablespoons
Tuna Fish	7 ounces	1-1/3 cups flaked

SUBSTITUTING NUMBER OF RETAIL CANS INTO INSTITUTIONAL NO. 10 CANS

7 No. 303	(1 lb.)	cans equal	1 No. 10 can
5 No. 2	(1 lb. 4 oz.)	cans equal	1 No. 10 can
4 No. 2-1/2	(1 lb. 13 oz.)	cans equal	1 No. 10 can
2 No. 3 Cyl.	(46 to 50 oz.)	cans equal	1 No. 10 can

	CONTAINER		
INDUSTRY TERM	CONSUMER DESCRIPTION		PRODUCTS
	Approximate Net Weight (check label)	Approximate Cups	
8 oz.	8 oz.	1	Fruits, vegetables, specialties*
Picnic	10-1/2 to 12 oz.	1-1/4	Condensed soups, small quantities of fruits, vegetables, meat and fish products, specialties*
12 oz. (vacuum)	12 oz.	1-1/2	Used largely for vacuum packed corn
No. 300	14 to 16 oz.	1-3/4	Pork and beans, baked beans, meat products, cranberry sauce, blueberries, specialties*
No. 303	16 to 17 oz.	2	Fruits, vegetables, meat products, ready-to-serve soups, specialties*
No. 2	1 lb. 4 oz. or 1 pt. 2 fl. oz.	2-1/2	Juices, ready-to-serve soups, specialties,* and a few fruits and vegetables
No. 2-1/2	1 lb. 13 oz.	3-1/2	Fruits, some vegetables (pumpkin, sauerkraut, spinach and other greens, tomatoes)
No. 3 Cyl.	3 lb. 3 oz. or 1 qt. 14 fl. oz.	5-3/4	Fruit and vegetable juices, pork and beans, condensed soup and some vegetables for institutional use
No. 5	56 oz.	7	Juice
No. 10	6-1/2 lb. to 7 lb. 5 oz.	12 to 13	Fruits, vegetables for restaurant and institutional use

*SPECIALTIES: Usually a food combination such as macaroni, spaghetti, Spanish style rice, Mexican type foods, Chinese foods, tomato aspic, etc.

FOOD BUYING GUIDE FOR DAY CARE CENTERS

Protein Foods

Food	Size of Standard Serving (cooked)	Servings, Per Unit Purchased	Amount to Buy to Serve 25
BEEF			
Ground	2 oz.	6 per lb.	4-1/2 lbs.
Stew Meat	2 oz.	6 per lb.	4-1/2 lbs.
Brisket, corned or fresh			
(bone-in)	2 oz.	4-1/2 per lb.	5-1/2 lbs.
(boneless)	2 oz.	5 per lb.	5 lbs.
Roasts, chuck (bone-in) round, rump, rib (bone-in)	1-1/2 to 2 oz.	5 per lb.	5 lbs.
Steak (boneless)	2 oz.	7 per lb.	3 lbs.
Liver	2 oz.	7 per lb.	3 lbs.
Dried Beef	2 oz.	10 per lb.	2-1/2 lbs.
PORK			
Ham, boneless (fresh or smoked)	2 oz.	5 per lb.	5 lbs.
Ham, bone-in (fresh or smoked)	2 oz.	3-1/2 per lb.	7 lbs.
Sausage, bulk	1 to 1-1/2 oz.	6 to 7 per lb.	3-1/2 lbs.
LAMB			
Chops, loin or rib	1 to 3 oz., chop	2 per lb.	12-1/2 lbs.

POULTRY			
Chicken, stewing (ready to cook)	2 oz.	3 per lb.	8 lbs.
Turkey, eviscerated	2 oz.	3-1/2 per lb.	7 lbs.
FISH			
Fillet, fresh or frozen (cod, haddock, ocean perch, pollock and whiting)	2 oz.	5 per lb.	5 lbs.
Canned Salmon or Mackerel	2 oz.	6-1/4 per lb.	4 lbs.
Tuna Fish	2 oz.	3 per lb. (6-1/2 oz. cans)	8 6-1/2 oz. cans
MISCELLANEOUS			
Luncheon meats (all meat)	1 oz.	16 per lb.	1-7/16 lbs.
	2 oz.	8 per lb.	3-1/4 lbs.
Weiners (all meat)	1 oz.	10 per lb.	2-1/2 to 3 lbs.
Cheese	2 oz.	8 per lb.	3-1/8 lbs.
Cheddar	1 oz.	16 per lb.	1-3/4 lbs.
Cottage	1/2 cup (equals 2 oz. of protein food)	4 per lb.	6-1/4 lbs.
	1/4 cup (equals 1 oz. of protein food)	8 per lb.	3-1/4 lbs.
Peanut Butter	2 tbs. (equals 1 oz. of protein food)	14 per lb.	1-3/4 lbs.
Dried Beans or Peas	1/2 cup (equals 2 oz. of protein food)	10 per lb.	2-1/2 lbs.
Eggs	1 egg (equals 1 oz. of protein food)	12 per doz.	2-1/12 doz.

FOOD BUYING GUIDE FOR DAY CARE CENTERS *(cont.)*

Fruits and Vegetables

Food	Size of Standard Serving	Servings, Per Unit Purchased	Amount to Buy to serve 25
FRESH FRUITS			
Apples	1 small	6 to 8 per lb.	3-1/2 lbs.
Bananas	1/2 med. or 1/4 cup sliced	3 per lb.	4 lbs.
Berries (blackberries, blueberries, raspberries, strawberries)	1/4 cup	10 per qt.	1 qt. + 1 pt.
Cantaloupe	1/8 (1/4 cup cubed)	8 (size 27 to 36)	3 to 4
Grapefruit (fresh)	1 half	2 each (size 70 to 96)	13
Grapes, seedless	1/4 cup,whole	10 per lb.	2-1/2 lbs.
Honeydew Melon	1/8 (1/4 cup cubed)	8	4
Oranges	1 small or 1/4 cup sections	12 per doz.	2-1/4 doz.
Peaches	1 small or 1/4 cup sliced	8 per lb.	3-1/4 lbs.
Pears	1 small	5 per lb.	5 lbs.
Plums	1 medium	10 med. per lb.	2-1/2 lbs.
Tangerines	1 small	6 per lb.	3-1/4 lbs.
Watermelon	1 slice or wedge or 1/4 cup cubed	2-1/2 per lb.	5 lbs.

FROZEN VEGETABLES			
Asparagus	1/4 cup	5 per 10 oz. pkg.	5 10 oz. pkg.
		26 per 2-1/2 lb. pkg.	1 2-1/2 lb. pkg.
Lima Beans	1/4 cup	5 per 10 oz. pkg.	5 10 oz. pkg.
		26 per 2-1/2 lb. pkg	1 2-1/2 lb. pkg.
Green Beans	1/4 cup	5 per 10 oz. pkg.	5 10 oz. pkg.
		26 per 1-1/2 lb. pkg	1 2-1/2 lb. pkg.
Brussel Sprouts	1/4 cup	6 per 12 oz. pkg.	4 12 oz. pkg.
		26 per 2-1/2 lb. pkg.	1 2-1/2 lb. pkg.
Broccoli	1/4 cup	6 per 12 oz. pkg.	4 12 oz. pkg.
		26 per 2-1/2 lb. pkg.	1 2-1/2 lb. pkg.
Cauliflower	1/4 cup	6 per 12 oz. pkg.	4 12 oz. pkg.
		26 per 2-1/2 lb. pkg.	1 2-1/2 lb. pkg.
Corn	1/4 cup	6 per 12 oz. pkg.	4 12 oz. pkg.
		26 per 2-1/2 lb. pkg.	1 2-1/2 lb. pkg.
Peas	1/4 cup	5 per 10 oz. pkg.	4 10 oz. pkg.
		26 per 2-1/2 lb. pkg.	1 2-1/2 lb. pkg.
Peas and Carrots	1/4 cup	5 per 10 oz. pkg.	4 10 oz. pkg.
		26 per 2-1/2 lb. pkg.	1 2-1/2 lb. pkg.
Spinach	1/4 cup	5 per 10 oz. pkg.	4 10 oz. pkg.
		26 per 2-1/2 lb. pkg.	1 2-1/2 lb. pkg.
Mixed Vegetables	1/4 cup	6 per 12 oz. pkg.	4 12 oz. pkg.
		26 per 2-1/2 lb. pkg.	1 2-1/2 lb. pkg.

FOOD BUYING GUIDE FOR DAY CARE CENTERS *(cont.)*

Fruits and Vegetables (cont.)

Food	Size of Standard Serving	Servings, Per Unit Purchased	Amount to Buy to Serve 25
CANNED FRUITS			
Apples	1/4 cup	8 per No. 303 can	3 No. 303 cans
		10 per No. 2 can	3 No. 2 cans
		14 per No. 2-1/2 can	2 No. 2-1/2 cans
		50 per No. 10 can	2 No. 10 cans
Applesauce	1/4 cup	Same as above	Same as above
Berries	1/4 cup	Same as above	Same as above
Cherries	1/4 cup	Same as above	Same as above
Grapes	1/4 cup	Same as above	Same as above
Grapefruit and Orange Sections	1/4 cup	Same as above	Same as above
Fruit Cocktail	1/4 cup	Same as above	Same as above
Fruits for Salad	1/4 cup	Same as above	Same as above
Peaches, sliced	1/4 cup	Same as above	Same as above
Pears	1 half	Same as above	Same as above
Pineapple Chunks	1/4 cup	Same as above	Same as above
Apricots	4 halves or 2 whole	5 per No. 2 can	5 No. 2 cans
		7 per No. 2-1/2 can	4 No. 2-1/2 cans
		25 per No. 10 can	1 No. 10 can

Grapefruit	1/2 cup	11-1/2 per 46 oz. can	3 46 oz. cans
Blended Grapefruit and Orange	1/2 cup	Same as above	Same as above
Orange	1/2 cup	Same as above	Same as above
Pineapple	1/2 cup	Same as above	Same as above
Tomato	1/2 cup	Same as above	Same as above
Vegetable Cocktail	1/2 cup	Same as above	Same as above
FROZEN FRUIT JUICES			
Grape	1/2 cup	6 per 6 oz. can	4-1/2 cans
		27 per 27 oz. can	1 can
		32 per 32 oz. can	3/4 can
Grapefruit	1/2 cup	Same as above	Same as above
Blended Grapefruit and Orange	1/2 cup	Same as above	Same as above
Pineapple	1/2 cup	Same as above	Same as above
Tangerine	1/2 cup	Same as above	Same as above
Grapefruit Sections	1/4 cup	8 per 1 lb. pkg.	3 pkgs.
		20 per 2-1/2 lb. pkg.	2 pkgs.
Peaches	1/4 cup	Same as above	Same as above
Strawberries	1/4 cup	Same as above	Same as above
FRESH VEGETABLES			
Asparagus	1/4 cup cooked	8 per lb.	3 lbs.
Beans, Snap or Wax	1/4 cup, cooked	9 per lb.	2-3/4 lbs.
Beets, fresh, no tops	1/4 cup, cooked	8 per lb.	3 lbs.
Broccoli	1/4 cup, cooked	6 per lb.	3 lbs.
Cabbage, green, red, or white, fresh	1/4 cup cooked	10 per lb.	2-1/2 lbs.
	1/4 cup, raw	12 per lb.	2-1/4 lbs.
Carrots, no tops	1/4 cup cooked	8 per lb.	3 lbs.
	1/4 cup, raw, shredded	12 per lb.	2-1/4 lbs.

FOOD BUYING GUIDE FOR DAY CARE CENTERS *(cont.)*

Fruits and Vegetables (cont.)

Food	Size of Standard Serving	Servings, Per Unit Purchased	Amount to Buy to serve 25
FRESH VEGETABLES (cont.)			
Cauliflower	1/4 cup, cooked	8 per lb.	3 lbs.
Chard or Kale	1/4 cup, cooked	7 per lb.	3-1/2 lbs.
Lettuce	1/4 cup, raw	10 med. per head	2 large or 3 small
Potatoes	1/4 cup, cooked	6 per lb.	3 lbs.
Spinach	1/4 cup, raw pieces	10	2-1/2 lbs.
	1/4 cup, cooked	6	4 lbs.
Squash, summer	1/4 cup, cooked	6	4 lbs.
Squash, winter	1/4 cup, cooked	6	4 lbs.
Sweet Potatoes	1/4 cup, cooked	6	4 lbs.
Tomatoes	1/4 cup, sliced or diced	10	2-1/2 lbs.
CANNED FRUITS			
Peach Halves	1 half	5 per No. 2 can	3 No. 2 cans
Pear Halves	1 half	14 per No. 2-1/2 can	2 No. 2-1/2 cans
		50 per No. 10 can	
Pineapple, sliced	1 slice	10 per No. 2 can	
		16 per No. 2-1/2 can	2 No. 2-1/2 cans
		50 per No. 10 can	
Plums, Prunes	2 whole	5 per No. 2 can	
		7 per No. 2-1/2 can	3-1/2 No. 2-1/2 cans

		100 per No. 10 can	
CANNED VEGETABLES			
Asparagus	1/4 cup	10 per No. 2 can	3 No. 2 cans
		14 per No. 2-1/2 can	3-1/2 No. 2-1/2 cans
		50 per No. 10 can	
Beans, Green or Wax	1/4 cup	Same as above	Same as above
Kidney Beans	1/4 cup	Same as above	Same as above
Beets	1/4 cup	Same as above	Same as above
Carrots	1/4 cup	Same as above	Same as above
Corn	1/4 cup	Same as above	Same as above
Peas	1/4 cup	Same as above	Same as above
Peas and Carrots	1/4 cup	Same as above	Same as above
Pumpkin	1/4 cup	Same as above	Same as above
Spinach	1/4 cup	Same as above	Same as above
Sweet Potatoes	1/4 cup	Same as above	Same as above
Tomatoes	1/4 cup	Same as above	Same as above
Mixed Vegetables	1/4 cup	Same as above	Same as above

Bread and Cereal Products

BREAD			
Raisin	1 slice	36/2 lb. loaves	1 loaf
Rye	1 slice	23/1 lb. loaves	2 loaves
		33/2 lb. loaves	1 loaf
White or Whole Wheat	1 slice	16/1 lb. loaves	2 loaves
		28/2 lb. loaves	1 loaf
Rolls	1	12 dozen	2-1/4 doz.

FOOD BUYING GUIDE FOR DAY CARE CENTERS *(cont.)*

Bread and Cereal Products (cont.)

Food	Size of Standard Serving (cooked)	Servings, Per Unit Purchased	Amount to Buy to Serve 25
CEREALS			
Dry	1/2 cup	12 oz. pkg.	
		18 oz. pkg.	
To Cook	1/2 cup, cooked	20/lb. cooked	1-1/2 lbs.
Rice	1/4 cup, cooked	32/lb. cooked	12 oz.
Macaroni	1/4 cup, cooked	36/lb. cooked	12 oz.
Noodles	1/4 cup, cooked	36/lb. cooked	12 oz.
Spaghetti	1/4 cup, cooked	36/lb. cooked	12 oz.
Dairy Products			
MILK			
Milk, fluid (whole)	1 cup (8 oz.)	1 per 1/2 pint	25
		4 per quart	6-1/4 qts.
		16 per gallon	2 gals.
Ice Cream	1/2 cup	8 per brick qt.	3-1/2 qts.
		25 per gal bulk	1 gal.
Butter or Margarine	1 teaspoon (per meal)	96 per lb.	1/4 lb.

Soups

GREEN SPLIT PEA SOUP

INGREDIENTS	25 PORTIONS 4 to 5 ounces/1 gal.	PORTIONS	PORTIONS	PROCEDURE
MARGARINE	1/4 cup			1. Melt margarine in heavy sauce pan or trunnion kettle, over medium heat.
ONION, diced	2 cups			2. Add onion, celery, and parsley, stirring frequently; cook five minutes.
CELERY, diced	3 cups			3. Add water, salt, sugar, pepper, split peas and ham bone. Bring to boiling. Skim foam from surface.
PARSLEY, diced	2 to 3 sprigs			4. Simmer for 1-1/2 to 2 hours until peas are "mush" soft. Remove ham bone.
WATER	1 gallon			5. Stir in chicken broth
SALT	2 tablespoons			6. Add hot milk; blend thoroughly.
SUGAR	2 teaspoons			7. Use 4 ounce ladle to portion.
PEPPER	1/4 teaspoon			
GREEN SPLIT PEAS	2 pounds			
HAM BONE	Optional			
CONDENSED CHICKEN BROTH, canned	20 to 24 ounces			
MILK, hot	1 quart			

NAVY BEAN SOUP WITH DICED HAM

INGREDIENTS	25 PORTIONS 4-5 oz./1 gal.	PORTIONS	PORTIONS	PROCEDURE
NAVY BEANS, dried	1 pound			1. Sort and wash beans. Soak overnight.
COLD WATER	1-3/4 quart			2. Add onions and diced bacon. Cook beans in water in which they soaked.
ONIONS, chopped fine	1 tablespoon			3. When beans are tender, add milk, salt, pepper and ham. Stir gently.
BACON ENDS, diced	1 ounce			4. Bring to simmering point. Stir gently.
MILK*	1/2 gallon			5. Use 4 ounce ladle to portion.
SALT	1 teaspoon			
PEPPER	Dash			
HAM, trimmed and diced	1 pound			
*Reconstituted dry milk powder may be used as follows:				
WATER	1/2 gallon			
NON-FAT DRY MILK SOLIDS	1-1/2 cup			

CREAM OF SPINACH SOUP

INGREDIENTS	25 PORTIONS 4-5 oz./1 gal.	PORTIONS	PORTIONS	PROCEDURE
SPINACH, FROZEN	3 pounds			1. Cook spinach.
MARGARINE	1/2 cup			2. Drain spinach, reserving juice. Finely chop spinach.
FLOUR	1/2 cup			3. Melt margarine at low temperature. Add flour slowly and blend to form roux. Cook without browning for five minutes.
MILK*, hot, and JUICE OFF SPINACH	3/4 gallon			4. Slowly add hot milk to roux, stirring until smoothness is obtained.
ONION, grated	2 tablespoons			5. Add the cooked spinach, onion, salt and pepper.
SALT	1-1/2 tablespoons			6. Use 4 ounce ladle to portion.
PEPPER	Dash			

*Reconstituted dry milk powder may be used as follows:

WATER and SPINACH JUICE	1/2 gallon
NON-FAT DRY MILK SOLIDS	1-1/2 cups

CREAM OF POTATO SOUP

INGREDIENTS	25 PORTIONS 4-5 oz./1 gal.	PORTIONS	PORTIONS	PROCEDURE
POTATOES, diced	3 pounds			1. Boil the potatoes, onions and celery in water until soft.
ONIONS, grated	1 medium			2. Melt margarine at low temperature. Add flour slowly and blend to form roux. Cook without browning for five minutes.
CELERY, chopped fine	1/2 cup			3. Slowly add hot milk to roux stirring until smoothness is obtained.
MARGARINE	3/4 cup			4. Add the cooked potatoes, celery, onion, and liquid to milk mixture. Blend well.
FLOUR	1/4 cup			5. Check seasoning. Add salt, pepper, celery salt.
MILK*, hot	1/2 gallon			6. Add parsley before serving.
SALT	2 tablespoons			7. Use 4 ounce ladle to portion
PEPPER	1/2 teaspoon			
CELERY SALT	1/2 teaspoon			
PARSLEY, chopped	1 teaspoon			

*Reconstituted dry milk powder may be used as follows:

WATER	1/2 gallon
NON-FAT DRY MILK SOLIDS	1-1/2 cups

BASIC CREAM SOUP BASE

INGREDIENTS	PORTIONS 1 gallon	PORTIONS	PORTIONS	PROCEDURE
WATER	1 gallon			1. Reconstitute milk powder.
NON-FAT DRY MILK SOLIDS	3 cups			2. Bring milk to boiling point—DO NOT SCORCH.
MARGARINE	1-1/2 cups (12 ounces)			3. Melt margarine over low heat. Gradually add flour to form a roux. Cook slowly for 5 minutes. DO NOT BROWN.
FLOUR	1-1/4 cups			4. Add hot milk to flour (roux). Add milk slowly—STIRRING—to form smooth base.
SALT	2 tablespoons			5. Add salt and pepper.
PEPPER	Dash			6. Combine with vegetable or meat to complete preparation.

CHILLED ORANGE SNACK SOUP

INGREDIENTS	25 PORTIONS 4 ounces	PORTIONS	PORTIONS	PROCEDURE
ORANGE JUICE PINEAPPLE JUICE CLOVES CORN STARCH SUGAR LEMON JUICE	2 quarts 3 cups 6 3 tablespoons 1 cup 2 cups			1. Combine orange juice, pineapple juice and cloves. Bring to boil. DO NOT BOIL. Remove cloves. 2. Combine sugar and corn starch, add a little hot juice and mix well. 3. Add remainder of hot juice and cook until thickened, stirring constantly. 4. Cool and add lemon juice. 5. Chill. 6. Serve as a snack or in hot weather as part of lunch.

FRUIT SOUP

INGREDIENTS	25 PORTIONS 5 ounces	PORTIONS	PORTIONS	PROCEDURE
WATER	1 quart			1. Bring water to a boil. Add sugar. Stir until dissolved.
SUGAR	1-1/2 cups			
SWEET RED CHERRIES, pitted and drained	1 No. 303 can			2. Add PITTED cherries, peaches, maraschino cherries, mandarin oranges, syrup and lemon juice.
PEACHES, CANNED, diced, drained	1 No. 303 can			3. Return to boil–reduce heat to a bare simmer while proceeding.
MARASCHINO CHERRIES, drained–pieces	6 oz. bottle			4. Bring orange juice to boil in another saucepan.
MANDARIN ORANGES and SYRUP	1 11 oz. can			5. Blend cornstarch and cold water and add to orange juice, stirring until thickened and smooth.
LEMON JUICE	3 tablespoons			
ORANGE JUICE	1-1/2 quarts			6. Combine with fruit mixture and blend well; be careful not to mash fruit.
COLD WATER	1 cup			
CORNSTARCH	3 tablespoons			7. Serve hot, or chill and serve cold.

INGREDIENTS	PORTIONS	PORTIONS	PORTIONS	PROCEDURE

INGREDIENTS	PORTIONS	PORTIONS	PORTIONS	PROCEDURE

Main Dishes

BAKED MACARONI AND CHEESE

Preheat oven to 375°F.

INGREDIENTS	25 PORTIONS No. 16 Scoop	PORTIONS	PORTIONS	PROCEDURE
WATER, boiling	2-1/2 quarts			1. Add macaroni, salt and salad oil to boiling water.
SALT	1 tablespoon			2. Cook until tender (about 10 minutes). DO NOT OVERCOOK.
SALAD OIL	1 tablespoon			3. Drain and rinse macaroni
MACARONI, RAW	12 ounces			4. Melt butter, slowly add (stirring) flour to form roux. Cook 5 minutes. DO NOT BROWN.
FLOUR	1/2 cup			5. Slowly add hot milk to form smooth sauce.
MILK, hot	1 quart			6. Add salt and cheese, mix well until cheese is melted.
SALT	2 teaspoons			7. Combine cheese sauce and macaroni.
CHEESE, grated	1 quart			8. Pour into greased baking pan.
MARGARINE	1/2 cup			9. Bake in oven at 375°F. for 15 to 20 minutes.
				10. Portion with No. 16 scoop.

CHEESE STRATA

Preheat oven to 325°F.

INGREDIENTS	25 PORTIONS	PORTIONS	PORTIONS	PROCEDURE
MARGARINE *OR* BUTTER	1-1/2 pounds			1. Spread bread on side as for sandwich.
BREAD, slices	50 slices			2. Place layer of bread (butter side down) in baking dish.
CHEESE, sliced (American or Processed)	25 (3/4 oz.)			3. Place 1 slice of cheese on each slice of bread.
EGGS	16 each			4. Top each with slice of buttered bread.
MILK	2-1/2 quarts			5. Beat eggs, add milk and salt.
SALT	1 tablespoon			6. Pour egg and milk mixture over sandwiches. Let stand 15 to 20 minutes.
				7. Bake at 325°F. for 40 minutes or until puffed up and brown.

CREAM COTTAGE CHEESE ENTREE OR SALAD

INGREDIENTS	25 PORTIONS No. 16 scoop	25 PORTIONS No. 24 scoop	PORTIONS	PROCEDURE
CREAM COTTAGE CHEESE	4 pounds	2 pounds		1. Combine cottage cheese and salt. 2. For plain cottage cheese, portion with scoop and place on lettuce. No. 16 Scoop (Entree). 3. Cottage cheese with fruit, portion with No. 24 scoop and combine with fruit of choice. (Salad)
SALT	2 teaspoons	1 teaspoon		
FRUIT:				
APRICOT	3 halves	75 halves or 1 No. 10 can		
OR				
FRUIT COCKTAIL, drained	No. 20 scoop	8 cups or 1 No. 10 can		
OR				
PEAR HALVES	1 half	25 halves or 1 No. 10 can		
OR				
PEACH HALVES	1 half	25 halves or 1 No. 10 can		
OR				
PINEAPPLE SLICES	1 slice	25 slices or 1 No. 10 can		
	ENTREE	**SALAD**		

INGREDIENTS	PORTIONS	PORTIONS	PORTIONS	PROCEDURE

INGREDIENTS	PORTIONS	PORTIONS	PORTIONS	PROCEDURE

BAKED OMELET

Preheat oven to 325°F.

INGREDIENTS	25 PORTIONS 2-1/2 ounces	PORTIONS	PORTIONS	PROCEDURE
MARGARINE	3/4 cup			1. Melt margarine over low heat. Stir in flour and cook slowly a few minutes without browning.
FLOUR	3/4 cup			
MILK, hot	1-1/2 quarts			2. Slowly (stirring) add hot milk to form smooth sauce.
SALT	1 tablespoon			3. Add salt and pepper and cool the sauce.
PEPPER	Dash			
EGG YOLKS, beaten	12 each			4. Add the beaten yolks. Mix well.
EGG WHITES, beaten stiff	12 each			5. Fold in egg whites.
				6. Pour mixture into well oiled 10-inch by 12-inch by 2-inch baking pan.
				7. Set pan in hot water, bake about 45 minutes at 325°F.
VARIATIONS	*ADD*			
BACON Crisp bacon, drained	1/2 cup			
CHEDDAR CHEESE, Grated	1/2 cup			
JELLY Tart jelly (apple) Spread over top of omelet before serving	1/2 cup			
HAM, diced	1/2 cup			

EGGS A LA KING

INGREDIENTS	25 PORTIONS 4-5 oz./1 gal.	PORTIONS	PORTIONS	PROCEDURE
MARGARINE	1 cup			1. Make white sauce by melting margarine at low temperature. Add flour slowly, stirring for about 5 minutes to form roux. Do not brown.
FLOUR	1-1/2 cups			2. Slowly add hot milk, stirring until smooth. Bring to a simmer.
SALT	1 tablespoon			3. Add worcestershire sauce, pimiento, and eggs.
PEPPER	Dash			4. Reheat to serving temperature.
MILK, hot	3 quarts			5. Portion with 4 ounce ladle over 1 slice toast or biscuit.
WORCESTERSHIRE SAUCE	1 teaspoon			
PIMIENTOS, chopped	1/2 cup			
EGGS, hard cooked (cut in quarters lengthwise)	2-1/2 dozen			
TOAST SLICES	25			

DEVILED EGGS

INGREDIENTS	25 PORTIONS 2 halves	PORTIONS	PORTIONS	PROCEDURE
HARD COOKED EGGS	25 each			1. Remove egg shells. Rinse under cold water.
SALAD DRESSING	1 cup			2. Cut eggs in half lengthwise. Remove yolks.
PREPARED MUSTARD	1 teaspoon			3. Mix salad dressing, mustard, salt and pepper.
SALT	1 teaspoon			4. Add dressing to egg yolks and mix well. (Put in blender, mixer or mash with fork until smooth.)
PEPPER	Dash			5. Fill egg whites with yolk mixture using pastry tube or teaspoon.
PAPRIKA				6. Sprinkle lightly with paprika for color interest.

EGG AND BACON LOAF

Preheat oven to 325°F.

INGREDIENTS	25 PORTIONS 3-1/2 ounces	PORTIONS	PORTIONS	PROCEDURE
BACON	1 pound			1. Coarsely chop bacon and fry until golden brown. Drain bacon.
MILK	1 quart + 1 cup			2. Pour milk over bread, add eggs and beat in mixer at low speed.
STALE BREAD, cubed	1 pound			3. Add bacon and remaining ingredients. Beat one minute to mix well.
EGGS	16 large			4. Pour into greased pan or casserole.
BACON FAT	2 tablespoons			5. Place pan in hot water.
SALT	1 tablespoon			6. Bake at 325°F. (slow) for 40 to 50 minutes.
ONION, grated	1 teaspoon			
PARSLEY, chopped	1/4 cup			
OR				
DRIED PARSLEY	1 teaspoon			
BAKING POWDER	2 teaspoons			

EGGS IN A NEST

INGREDIENTS	25 PORTIONS	PORTIONS	PORTIONS	PROCEDURE
BREAD	25 slices			1. Remove center from bread slices with biscuit cutter.*
MARGARINE *OR* BUTTER	1/2 pound			2. Melt margarine.
EGGS	25 each			3. After circles are removed, brush bread slices with melted butter.
SALT				4. Cook bread on grill until brown and crisp on one side.
				5. Brush top side of bread with margarine, turn bread.
				6. Crack one egg into each "hole." Salt lightly. Cook over low heat until egg is done.
				7. Serve immediately.

*Bread circles can be used for pizzaburgers.

EGG FOO YONG

INGREDIENTS	25 PORTIONS 2-1/2 ounces	PORTIONS	PORTIONS	PROCEDURE
GREEN ONIONS (including tops) BEAN SPROUTS, CANNED, drained CORNSTARCH SALT PEPPER WHOLE EGGS SHORTENING	1-1/4 bunch (3 cups) 2 to 2-1/2 cans 1/2 cup 1/2 teaspoon 1/2 teaspoon 13 each			1. Wash, trim and chop onions in approximately 1/4 inch pieces. 2. Combine chopped onions, drained bean sprouts, cornstarch, salt, and pepper. 3. Mix eggs just enough to combine yolks and whites. 4. Pour eggs over bean sprouts and mix by hand. 5. Heat grill or skillet to medium heat (350°F.); melt shortening. 6. Use No. 12 scoop or 3 ounce ladle to portion. Grill until brown and turn and brown other side. 7. Serve with Soy Gravy. (See recipe next page.)

SOY GRAVY

INGREDIENTS	25 PORTIONS 1/2 ounce	PORTIONS	PORTIONS	PROCEDURE
WATER	1-1/3 cups			1. Combine water, soy sauce, and liquid gravy browning. Bring to boil.
SOY SAUCE	2 tablespoons + 2 teaspoons			
LIQUID GRAVY BROWNING	1/2 teaspoon			
CORNSTARCH	2 tablespoons			2. Mix cornstarch with cold water. Add to above and cook (stirring continually) until clear and slightly thickened.
COLD WATER	3 tablespoons			3. Serve with Egg Foo Yong.

INGREDIENTS	PORTIONS	PORTIONS	PORTIONS	PROCEDURE

INGREDIENTS	PORTIONS	PORTIONS	PORTIONS	PROCEDURE

INGREDIENTS	PORTIONS	PORTIONS	PORTIONS	PROCEDURE

CHEESE STUFFED FRANKFURTERS

Preheat oven to 350°F.

INGREDIENTS	25 PORTIONS	PORTIONS	PORTIONS	PROCEDURE
CHEDDAR CHEESE, grated	6 ounces			1. Coarsely grate cheddar cheese.
SWEET PICKLE RELISH	1/2 cup			2. Combine cheese, pickle relish, and salt.
SALT	1/4 teaspoon			3. Split frankfurters lengthwise, not quite through.
FRANKFURTERS (10 to a pound)	25 each			4. Stuff frankfurters with cheese mixture.
				5. Place frankfurters, cheese side up, on bun pan.
				6. Bake 20 to 25 minutes until cheese is bubbly.

BREAD STUFFED FRANKFURTERS

Preheat oven to 350°F.

INGREDIENTS	25 PORTIONS	PORTIONS	PORTIONS	PROCEDURE
BREAD CRUMBS	3 cups			1. Split frankfurters lengthwise, not quite through.
ONIONS, minced	1 cup			2. Spread split frankfurters with thin layer of catsup.
SALT	1 teaspoon			3. Combine bread crumbs, minced onions, salt, margarine, and milk.
MARGARINE *OR* BUTTER	3/4 cup			4. Cover frankfurters with bread mixture.
MILK	1/2 cup			5. Place on bun pan and bake 25 to 30 minutes or until crumb mixture is golden brown.
FRANKFURTERS (10 per 1 pound)	25 each			
CATSUP				

CHILI CON CARNE

INGREDIENTS	25 5oz. PORTIONS 1 gallon	PORTIONS	PORTIONS	1. PROCEDURE
DRY CHILI BEANS (Pinto or Kidney)	12 ounces			1. Sort beans, wash and cook (with onion) 2 hours or until tender but still firm. Remove onion. Drain.
WATER	2 quarts			
ONION, whole, peeled	1 large			
SHORTENING	2/3 cup			2. Heat shortening, add onion, pepper and bacon. Saute until golden brown.
ONION, chopped	1/2 cup			
GREEN PEPPER, chopped	1 each			
BACON, finely chopped	2 slices			
BEEF, LEAN, coarsely ground	2-1/2 pounds			3. Add ground beef and chili powder. Stir occasionally until lightly browned.
CHILI POWDER	2 teaspoons			
TOMATOES, CANNED, chopped	1-1/2 quarts			4. Add tomatoes, juice and spices. Bring to a boil and simmer for 30 minutes. Skim off fat.
TOMATO JUICE	3 cups			
SUGAR	1-1/2 tablespoons			
SALT	2 tablespoons			
PAPRIKA	1 tablespoon			
BLACK PEPPER	1/4 teaspoon			
MONOSODIUM GLUTAMATE	1 teaspoon			5. Add drained, cooked beans just to heat. Serve.

PORK-APPLE CASSEROLE WITH MASHED SWEET POTATO TOPPING

Preheat oven to 450°F.

INGREDIENTS	25 PORTIONS 4 ounces	PORTIONS	PORTIONS	PROCEDURE
SHORTENING	1 tablespoon			1. Brown pork cubes in shortening.
PORK CUBES (approx. 40 per pound)	2-1/2 pounds			2. Add onions. Add hot water. Cover. Simmer 20 minutes.
ONION, chopped	1 small			3. Add seasonings. Cover, simmer 10 to 15 minutes more or until meat is tender.
HOT WATER				4. Make paste of flour and water. (Strain if lumpy.) Add to meat mixture, cooking and stirring gently 5 to 7 minutes until thickened and cooked.
SALT	1 tablespoon			5. Add halved apple slices; stir.
DRY MUSTARD	1 teaspoon			6. Place pork/apple mixture in lightly buttered baking pan.
BLACK PEPPER	1/4 teaspoon			7. Top with mashed sweet potato topping. Sprinkle with margarine and brown sugar. Bake at 450°F. until hot.
MONOSODIUM GLUTAMATE	1/2 teaspoon			
LIQUID GRAVY BROWNING	1/2 teaspoon			
COLD WATER	3/4 cup			
FLOUR	1/2 cup			
SLICED APPLES, CANNED, halved	No. 2-1/2 can			
SWEET POTATOES	3-1/2 pounds			

SWEET POTATO TOPPING

Pare and parboil sweet potatoes and mash, or use Instant Mashed Sweet Potato Flakes.

BARBECUED GROUND BEEF

INGREDIENTS	25 PORTIONS 2 ounces	PORTIONS	PORTIONS	PROCEDURE
ONIONS, chopped	2 cups			1. Saute chopped onions in small amount of fat until transparent.
GROUND BEEF	3 pounds			2. Add ground beef and cook slowly until beef loses its red color.
CHICKEN BASE *OR* BOUILLON CUBES	1 ounce			3. Drain juice off meat, skim fat off liquid and discard.
PREPARED MUSTARD	1/2 cup			4. Dissolve chicken base in beef liquid and return to meat.
CATSUP	1/2 cup			5. Add mustard, catsup, and spices. Stir well.
SALT	1 tablespoon			6. Serve with No. 16 scoop or 2 ounce ladle—ON BUN.
PEPPER	1/4 teaspoon			
MONOSODIUM GLUTAMATE	1/4 teaspoon			

PIZZA BURGERS

Preheat oven to 425°F.

INGREDIENTS	25 PORTIONS 25 1 bun half, No. 20 scoop	PORTIONS	PORTIONS	PROCEDURE
GROUND BEEF	2-1/2 pounds			1. Brown beef and onions.
ONION, chopped	2 tablespoons			2. Add salt, oregano, celery, and pepper to meat.
SALT	1/2 teaspoon			3. Add tomato puree and grated cheddar cheese. Cook until cheese melts and mixture is of medium thickness.
OREGANO	Dash			4. Portion with No. 20 scoop on open bun half or English muffin half. Or portion with No. 40 scoop on bread circles.
CELERY, chopped	2 tablespoons			5. Spread meat mixture and sprinkle with parmesan cheese.
PEPPER	Dash			6. Bake at 425°F. until cheese melts.
TOMATO PUREE	2 8 ounce cans			7. Serve 1 bun half, or 1 English muffin half or 2 bread circles per portion.
CHEDDAR CHEESE, grated	3/4 pound (3 cups)			
PARMESAN CHEESE, grated	4 ounces (1 cup)			
ROUND BUNS *OR* ENGLISH MUFFINS	13			

AU GRATIN HAM AND POTATOES

Preheat oven to 350°F.

INGREDIENTS	25 PORTIONS 3-1/2 ounces	PORTIONS	PORTIONS	PROCEDURE
POTATOES, sliced thin	3 pounds			1. Wash, peel and thinly slice potatoes.
MARGARINE *OR* BUTTER	1/4 cup			2. Place potatoes in greased baking pan.
FLOUR	1/2 cup			3. Melt margarine over low heat, slowly (stirring) add flour to form roux. Cook for approximately 5 minutes—DO NOT BROWN.
MILK	1 quart			4. Slowly add milk (stirring) to form smooth cream sauce.
SALT	2 teaspoons			5. Add salt and cheese and stir until cheese melts.
CHEDDAR CHEESE, grated	2 cups			6. Evenly distribute ham over potatoes.
HAM, cubed	2 quarts			7. Pour cheese sauce over ham and potatoes.
BREAD CRUMBS	2 cups			8. Top with buttered crumbs.
MARGARINE *OR* BUTTER	1/4 cup			9. Bake at 350°F. for 1 hour or until potatoes are fork tender.

BOLOGNA CUP WITH BAKED BEANS

Preheat oven to 350°F.

INGREDIENTS	25 PORTIONS	PORTIONS	PORTIONS	PROCEDURE
BOLOGNA	25 1 ounce slices			1. Brush muffin tins with melted margarine.
MARGARINE, melted	1/2 cup			2. Place a bologna slice inside of muffin tin (or individual casserole or custard cup).
BAKED BEANS, CANNED	2 No. 3 cyl. cans (11-1/2 cups)			3. Combine beans, catsup, mustard, brown sugar and onions.
CATSUP	1 cup			4. Portion beans with No. 16 scoop and fill bologna cup.
PREPARED MUSTARD	1/4 cup			5. Bake in oven at 350°F. for 45 minutes.
BROWN SUGAR	1/2 cup			
ONION, chopped	1/4 cup			

CHICKEN AND RICE CASSEROLE

Preheat oven to 350°F.

INGREDIENTS	25 PORTIONS	PORTIONS	PORTIONS	PROCEDURE
STEWING HENS *OR* COOKED CHICKEN, diced	2 large or 2 quarts			1. Stew chicken, cut meat in small pieces.
COOKED RICE	3 cups			2. Combine chicken, rice, onion and place in greased baking pan.
ONION, chopped	1/4 cup			3. Sprinkle with grated cheese.
CHEDDAR CHEESE, grated	8 ounces (2 cups)			4. Combine mushroom and chicken soup to make sauce. Pour over casserole.
MUSHROOM SOUP	2 10-3/4 ounce cans			5. Bake at 350°F. for 1 hour.
CHICKEN SOUP	2 10-3/4 ounce cans			

SPAGHETTI SAUCE WITH BEEF

INGREDIENTS	25 PORTIONS 3 ounces	PORTIONS	PORTIONS	PROCEDURE
ONION, chopped	3/4 cup			1. Brown onion and garlic in oil until onions are transparent.
GARLIC CLOVES, minced	3 each			2. Add ground beef and cook (stirring) until brown.
COOKING OIL	1/4 cup			3. Add puree, juice, tomatoes, sugar, salt, oregano, nutmeg, and carrots.
GROUND BEEF	3 pounds			4. Simmer mixture, stirring occasionally for about 2 hours.
TOMATO PUREE	3 cups			5. Serve over spaghetti, macaroni, noodles, or rice.
TOMATOES, CANNED	1 No. 2-1/2 can			
TOMATO JUICE	1 No. 5 can			
SUGAR	1/4 cup			
SALT	2 tablespoons			
OREGANO	2 teaspoons			
NUTMEG	1/2 teaspoon			
CARROTS, grated or diced finely	1 cup			

LIVER CASSEROLE WITH RICE

Preheat oven to 350°F.

INGREDIENTS	25 PORTIONS	PORTIONS	PORTIONS	PROCEDURE
LIVER	3 pounds			1. Cut liver into 1/2 inch strips.
FLOUR	1/2 cup			2. Dredge in flour–saute in oil until brown. Remove liver from frying pan.
COOKING OIL	1/2 cup			3. Saute onion and green pepper until tender.
ONIONS, chopped	1 cup			4. Combine all ingredients in a greased 17-inch by 24-inch by 2-inch baking pan.
GREEN PEPPERS, chopped	1 cup			5. Bake in oven at 350°F. for 40 minutes.
COOKED RICE	10 cups			
TOMATOES, CANNED	4 No. 2 cans (10 cups)			
SALT	1-1/2 tablespoons			
PEPPER	1/2 teaspoon			

BEEF AND NOODLE CASSEROLE

Preheat oven to 350°F.

INGREDIENTS	25 PORTIONS 4-5 ounces	PORTIONS	PORTIONS	PROCEDURE
BEEF, cooked and diced	3 pounds			1. Cook noodles in salted boiling water until tender.
NOODLES, MEDIUM	8 ounces			2. Drain noodles.
SHORTENING *OR* MARGARINE	1/2 cup			3. Melt shortening, slowly (stirring) add flour to form roux. Cook 5 minutes, do not brown. Slowly (stirring) add stock to form smooth sauce. Cook until thickened—add catsup and salt.
FLOUR	3/4 cup			4. Combine noodles and meat, place in greased 10-inch by 14-inch by 2-inch baking pan evenly; pour sauce over mixture.
BEEF STOCK *OR* BROTH	1-1/2 quarts			5. Sprinkle crumbs over top and brush with melted margarine.
CATSUP	1/4 cup			6. Bake at 350°F. for 1 hour.
SALT	1 teaspoon			
BREAD CRUMBS *OR* CRACKER CRUMBS	1/4 cup			
MARGARINE, melted	1/4 cup			

SEVEN LAYER CASSEROLE

Preheat oven to 350°F.

INGREDIENTS	25 PORTIONS 4-1/2 ounces	PORTIONS	PORTIONS	PROCEDURE
RICE, uncooked	3 cups			1. Grease 12-inch by 14-inch by 4-inch baking pan.
WHOLE KERNEL CORN, CANNED, drained	2 No. 2 cans			2. Place uncooked rice in bottom of pan.
SALT	1 teaspoon			3. Cover rice with drained whole kernel corn.
PEPPER	Dash			4. Sprinkle with salt and pepper
TOMATO SAUCE	3 8 ounce cans			5. Combine tomato sauce and water and cover corn layer.
WATER	12 ounces			6. Add onion and green pepper.
ONIONS, chopped	1-1/2 cups			7. Season ground beef with salt and pepper and evenly layer on top of onion and pepper.
GREEN PEPPERS, chopped	1-1/2 cups			8. Combine tomato sauce and water and pour over ground beef.
GROUND BEEF	2-1/2 pounds			9. Top with bacon strips.
SALT	2 teaspoons			10. Cover with foil. Bake at 350°F. for 1 hour. Uncover and return to oven for 30 minutes.
PEPPER	Dash			
TOMATO SAUCE	3 8 ounce cans			
WATER	6 ounces			
BACON	12 slices (cut in half)			

SPANISH LIVER

Preheat oven to 350°F.

INGREDIENTS	25 PORTIONS 2+ ounces	PORTIONS	PORTIONS	PROCEDURE
YOUNG BEEF LIVER	3 pounds			1. Cut liver in finger size pieces.
FLOUR	1/2 cup			2. Flour liver.
SHORTENING	1/4 cup			3. Brown liver in shortening.
TOMATOES, CANNED	1 No. 2-1/2 can			4. Place liver in greased baking pan.
SALT	2 teaspoons			5. Combine tomatoes, salt, pepper, onions, and green pepper. Pour over liver.
PEPPER	Dash			6. Bake at 350°F. for 40 minutes.
ONION, chopped	1/4 cup			
GREEN PEPPER, chopped	1/4 tablespoon			

LIVER LOAF

Preheat oven to 350°F.

INGREDIENTS	25 PORTIONS 2-1/2 ounces	PORTIONS	PORTIONS	PROCEDURE
LIVER, ground	1-1/2 pounds			1. Have butcher grind the liver and beef together.
BEEF, ground	1-1/2 pounds			2. Combine meat, onions, celery, parsley, salt, eggs, milk and dried bread crumbs or oatmeal.
ONION, chopped	1/2 cup			3. Mix well.
CELERY, chopped	1/2 cup			4. Shape into two loaves. Bake in greased baking pan at 350°F. for 1 hour.
PARSLEY, dried	1/2 teaspoon			5. Slice 2-1/2 ounces per serving.
SALT	1 tablespoon plus 1 teaspoon			
EGGS	3 each			
MILK	3 cups			
DRIED BREAD CRUMBS *OR* OATMEAL	2 cups			

TAMALE PIE

Preheat oven to 375°F.

INGREDIENTS	25 PORTIONS	PORTIONS	PORTIONS	PROCEDURE
WATER	1 gallon			1. Bring water to boil. Add salt. Stir in corn meal slowly. Cook 1 hour over low heat—stirring often to prevent lumping. Cool.
SALT	1 tablespoon + 1 teaspoon			
CORN MEAL	1 quart			
MARGARINE	1/2 cup			2. Brown onion and green pepper in fat. Crumble ground beef into mixture and brown.
ONION, chopped	1/2 cup			
GREEN PEPPER, chopped	1 small			
GROUND BEEF	2 pounds			
TOMATOES, CANNED	2 No. 2 cans			3. Add tomatoes and salt to meat mixture. Simmer 15 minutes.
SALT	1/2 tablespoon			
				4. Place 1/2 of cooked corn meal in bottom of greased baking pan.
MARGARINE, melted	1/4 cup			5. Add meat mixture—top with remaining corn meal. Brush with melted margarine.
				6. Bake at 375°F. for 1 hour.

CREAMED CHIPPED BEEF

INGREDIENTS	25 PORTIONS 4+ ounces	PORTIONS	PORTIONS	PROCEDURE
DRIED CHIPPED BEEF SHORTENING FLOUR MILK, hot PEPPER TOAST	2-1/2 pounds 1 cup 1 cup 1 gallon Dash 25 slices			1. Soak beef in water, drain, rinse, drain. 2. Melt shortening, stirring slowly; add flour to form roux. 3. Cook for 5 minutes. Do not brown. 4. Slowly (stirring) add hot milk to form smooth sauce. 5. Add drained chipped beef, stir and cook on low heat for 10 minutes. Add pepper. 6. Portion with 4 ounce ladle over toast.

Preheat oven to 350°F.

INGREDIENTS	25 PORTIONS No. 20 scoop	PORTIONS	PORTIONS	PROCEDURE
BEEF CUBES *OR* PORK CUBES	2-1/4 pounds			1. Brown meat cubes in cooking oil.
COOKING OIL (PEANUT)	2 tablespoons			2. Transfer meat into roasting pan. Add salt, bouillon, soy sauce and molasses. Cover. Bake at 350°F. for 1 hour.
SALT	2 teaspoons			3. Mix flour and water to form a "slur." Stir into meat. Add peppers, onions, and celery. Return to oven. Cook uncovered for 1 hour. Stir every 20 minutes.
CHICKEN BROTH, canned	2 cans			4. Add bean sprouts and mushrooms. Continue cooking for another 1/2 hour.
SOY SAUCE	1/2 cup			5. Cook rice and drain.
BEAD MOLASSES	1/4 cup			6. Serve chop suey over rice.
FLOUR	1/2 cup			
WATER	1 cup			
GREEN PEPPER, chopped	1 pepper			
ONION, chopped	1/4 cup			
CELERY, chopped	1 pint (1/2 bunch)			
BEAN SPROUTS	2 to 2-1/2 cans			
MUSHROOMS	1 8 ounce can			
RICE	1 pound			
WATER	2 quarts			

ROAST LOIN OF PORK

Preheat oven to 350°F.

INGREDIENTS	25 PORTIONS 2+ ounces	PORTIONS	PORTIONS	PROCEDURE
LOIN OF PORK, boneless	4 pounds			1. Season roast.
SALT	1 tablespoon			2. Place roast in roasting bag according to manufacturer's direction.
PEPPER	Dash			3. Place in roasting pan.
ROSEMARY	1/4 teaspoon			4. Bake for approximately 2 hours at 350°F.
ROASTING BAG				5. Remove roast—let set up for 20 minutes and slice.
				NOTE: Good served with apple dishes.

SWISS STEAK WITH VEGETABLE GRAVY

Preheat oven to 300°F.

INGREDIENTS	PORTIONS 2-1/2 ounces	PORTIONS	PORTIONS	PROCEDURE
ROUND STEAK, 1 inch thick	4 pounds			1. Cut steak in approximately 2-1/2 ounce pieces.
FLOUR	1/3 cup			2. Combine flour, salt and pepper. Dredge steak pieces.
SALT	1 tablespoon			3. Brown steak pieces on both sides in oil. Place steak in roasting pan.
PEPPER	Dash			4. Simmer broth, puree, soy sauce and bay leaf.
OIL	1/4 cup			5. Saute vegetables in oil. Add flour, stirring to form roux.
BEEF BROTH *OR* BOUILLON	2 cups			6. Remove bay leaf. Slowly add broth to roux, stirring to make vegetable gravy. Stirring, cook until smooth.
TOMATO PUREE	1 8 ounce can			7. Pour gravy over steak.
SOY SAUCE	1 tablespoon			8. Bake for approximately 1-1/2 hours until tender.
BAY LEAF				
OIL	1/4 cup			
CELERY, diced	1/2 cup			
ONION, diced	1/4 cup			
CARROT, diced	1/4 cup			
FLOUR	1/4 cup			

MEAT LOAF

Preheat oven to 350°F.

INGREDIENTS	25 PORTIONS 2 ounces	PORTIONS	PORTIONS	PROCEDURE
GROUND BEEF SALT PEPPER EGGS TOMATO PUREE OATMEAL	3 pounds 1 tablespoon 1/2 teaspoon 3 each 1 8 ounce can 1 cup			1. Combine all ingredients. 2. Shape meat mixture into 2 loaves. 3. Place in lightly greased roasting pans. 4. Bake at 350°F. for approximately 1-1/2 hours. 5. After 30 minutes and again after 60 minutes baking time pour off excess drippings (may be saved for making gravy). 6. Portion into 2 ounce servings.

ITALIAN MEAT BALLS

Preheat oven to 350°F.

INGREDIENTS	25 PORTIONS 3 No. 40 Scoops	PORTIONS	PORTIONS	PROCEDURE
GROUND BEEF *OR* 1/3 GROUND BEEF, PORK, AND VEAL	3 pounds			1. Saute onions and celery in oil. 2. Combine bread and broth or milk with bread cubes. 3. Add all remaining ingredients. 4. Using No. 40 scoop as a measuring guide, portion meat balls. 5. Place meat balls in greased baking pan. 6. Bake at 350°F. for approximately 20 to 25 minutes. 7. Serve plain or add to spaghetti sauce, brown gravy, mushroom gravy, etc.
ONIONS, finely chopped	2 cups			
CELERY, finely chopped	1 cup			
SALAD OIL	1/4 cup			
BREAD CUBES, FRESH	3 cups			
BROTH *OR* MILK	1/3 cup			
EGGS	2 each			
PARMESAN CHEESE, grated	1/4 cup			
PARSLEY, DRIED	2 teaspoons			
OREGANO	1/2 teaspoon			
SALT	1 tablespoon			
PEPPER	1/2 teaspoon			

POT ROAST WITH VEGETABLES

Preheat oven to 350°F.

INGREDIENTS	25 PORTIONS 2 ounces	PORTIONS	PORTIONS	PROCEDURE
BEEF ROAST, RUMP, CHUCK *OR* ROUND	5 pounds			1. Season meat.
SALT	2 tablespoons			2. Wash, pare, and cut vegetables into serving pieces.
PEPPER	1 teaspoon			3. Place roast, vegetables, water and worcestershire sauce in cooking/roasting bag; close lightly or according to manufacturer's direction.
CARROTS, RAW	3 pounds			4. Place in roasting pan.
POTATOES, RAW	3 pounds			5. Roast for approximately 1 hour and 45 minutes.
ONIONS, PEARL, CANNED	2 No. 2 cans			
CELERY, RAW	1/2 bunch			
WATER	1 cup			
WORCESTERSHIRE SAUCE	2 tablespoons			
ROASTING BAG	1 large (turkey size)			

BEEF STEAK PATTIES

Preheat oven to 350°F.

INGREDIENTS	25 PORTIONS 2+ ounces	PORTIONS	PORTIONS	PROCEDURE
BEEF, ground	3 lbs.			1. Combine all ingredients.
ONION, chopped	1/4 cup			2. Portion with No. 16 scoop and shape into patties.
SALT	2 teaspoons			3. Place on large greased baking pan.
PEPPER	Dash			4. Bake in oven at 350°F. for approximately 40 minutes.
WORCESTERSHIRE SAUCE	1 tablespoon			
EGGS	3 each			
OATMEAL *OR* BREAD CRUMBS *OR* ROLLED WHEAT	1 cup			

TURKEY PIE WITH BISCUIT TOPPING

Preheat oven to 450°F.

INGREDIENTS	25 PORTIONS 4+ ounces	PORTIONS	PORTIONS	PROCEDURE
TURKEY, diced and cooked	3 quarts or 3 pounds			1. Cook celery in canned chicken broth until tender.
CELERY, diced	1/2 cup			2. Drain and save liquid from canned carrots, peas, and potatoes.
CARROTS, cooked or canned	2 cups or 1 No. 303 can			3. Melt margarine, add flour slowly (stirring) to form roux. Cook for 5 minutes. DO NOT BROWN.
PEAS, CANNED	1 No. 303 can			4. Combine chicken broth, vegetable juice (and water if necessary) to make 1-1/4 quarts of liquid. Add slowly to roux to form smooth sauce. Add seasonings.
CHICKEN BROTH	2 No. 2 cans			5. Combine turkey, vegetables and sauce; pour in greased baking pan.
MARGARINE	1/4 cup			6. Top with biscuits, bake at 450°F. for 15 to 20 minutes until biscuits are brown.
FLOUR	1/2 cup			
SALT	1 tablespoon			
PEPPER	Dash			
ONION, chopped	2 tablespoons			
POTATOES, diced (cooked, canned or dehydrated)	1 quart			
BISCUITS, refrigerated	3 tubes			

THERESA CHILI PIE

Preheat oven to 350°F.

INGREDIENTS	25 PORTIONS	PORTIONS	PORTIONS	PROCEDURE
CORN BREAD *OR* TORTILLA CHIPS	2 quarts or 2 packages (7 ounce size)			1. Line a greased baking pan with crumbled corn bread or tortilla chips.
SHORTENING	2 tablespoons			2. Brown ground beef.
GROUND BEEF	2 pounds			3. Combine beef, beans, tomato paste, water, salt, chili powder, paprika and sugar.
KIDNEY *OR* PINTO BEANS, CANNED	2 No. 2-1/2 cans			4. Ladle beef mixture over corn bread or chips.
TOMATO PASTE	2 cups (2 8 ounce cans)			5. Layer chopped green onions.
WATER	1/2 cup			6. Layer tomatoes.
SALT	1 tablespoon			7. Top with grated cheese.
CHILI POWDER	2 teaspoons			8. Bake at 350°F. for 1 hour.
PAPRIKA	2 teaspoons			
SUGAR	1/4 cup			
GREEN ONIONS, chopped including green stems	1 to 2 bunches			
FRESH TOMATOES, diced	1 pint			
CHEESE, grated (Cheddar or Parmesan)	1 quart or 1 pound			

ENCHILADA PIE

Preheat oven to 400°F.

INGREDIENTS	25 PORTIONS	PORTIONS	PORTIONS	PROCEDURE
GROUND BEEF	2 pounds			1. Brown ground beef and onion.
ONION, chopped	1/4 cup			2. Add seasonings and tomato sauce.
SALT	2 teaspoons			3. Butter tortillas and cut in quarters.
CHILI POWDER	1 tablespoon			4. In a **greased baking pan, alternate** layers of buttered tortillas, meat sauce, olives, and cheese.
TOMATO SAUCE	2 8 ounce cans			
TORTILLAS, soft	12 each			
MARGARINE	1/4 cup			5. Add water and cover and bake at 400°F. for 20 minutes.
CHOPPED OLIVES	1 4-1/4 ounce can			
CHEDDAR CHEESE, grated	1 quart or 1 pound			6. Cut in wedges with sharp knife and serve.
WATER	2 cups			

INGREDIENTS	PORTIONS	PORTIONS	PORTIONS	PROCEDURE

INGREDIENTS	PORTIONS	PORTIONS	PORTIONS	PROCEDURE

INGREDIENTS	PORTIONS	PORTIONS	PORTIONS	PROCEDURE

CHILIBURGERS

INGREDIENTS	25 PORTIONS No. 20 Scoop	PORTIONS	PORTIONS	PROCEDURE
KIDNEY BEANS, DRY *OR* CANNED	1 cup or 2 No. 2-1/2 cans			1. Soak dry beans over night. Cook 1-1/2 to 2 hours.
SHORTENING	1/4 cup			2. Brown onion and ground beef in shortening.
ONION, chopped	1/4 cup			3. Add water and seasonings (Items 5 through 12) and simmer 15 minutes.
GROUND BEEF	1-3/4 pounds			4. Mash beans. Add beans and tomato paste to meat mixture.
WATER	1 cup			5. Combine flour and water to form "slur." Combine with meat mixture. Stir and cook until thickened.
SALT	1 tablespoon			6. Portion with No. 20 scoop.
CHILI POWDER	2 teaspoons			
MUSTARD, DRY	1 teaspoon			
VINEGAR	2 tablespoons			
CATSUP	1 cup			
PAPRIKA	2 teaspoons			
SUGAR	1/4 cup			
TOMATO PASTE	1 cup (1 8-ounce can)			
FLOUR	4 tablespoons			
WATER	1/2 cup			
BUNS (2-1/2 inch)	25 each			

SUBMARINE SANDWICHES

INGREDIENTS	25 PORTIONS	PORTIONS	PORTIONS	PROCEDURE
FRANKFURTER BUNS *OR* HAMBURGER BUNS (3 inch)	25 each			1. Open buns, spread with margarine. 2. Combine mayonnaise with finely chopped lettuce. 3. Place chopped lettuce on bottom half of buns, add one slice bologna and one slice cheese. 4. Top with sliced egg. 5. Add top half of bun—cut in half. 6. Serve 2 halves per serving.
MARGARINE	1 cup			
MAYONNAISE	1-1/2 cups			
LETTUCE, chopped	1/2 head			
BOLOGNA SLICES	25 3/4-ounce slices			
CHEESE SLICES (American—Pimiento—Mild Cheddar—or Swiss)	25 3/4-ounce slices			
HARD COOKED EGGS, sliced	9 each			

PEANUT BUTTER AND RAISIN SPREAD SANDWICH

INGREDIENTS	25 PORTIONS No. 20 Scoop	PORTIONS	PORTIONS	PROCEDURE
PEANUT BUTTER	3-1/2 cups (1 lb. 12 oz.)			1. Chop raisins. 2. Cream peanut butter and add 1 cup of fruit juice, add additional juice as required to make peanut butter mixture to desired spreading consistency. 3. Portion with No. 20 scoop. 4. Cut sandwiches in quarters or thirds for little fingers to handle.
RAISINS, chopped	2 cups (1 lb.)			
ANY FRUIT JUICE	1 cup to 2 cups			
BREAD	50 slices			
MARGARINE	1/2 pound			

EGG SALAD SANDWICH

INGREDIENTS	25 PORTIONS No. 16 scoop	PORTIONS	PORTIONS	PROCEDURE
HARD COOKED EGGS MAYONNAISE SWEET PICKLE RELISH SALT BREAD MARGARINE	25 each 1 cup 1 cup 2 teaspoons 50 slices 1/2 pound			1. Remove egg shells. Rinse under cold water. 2. Slice and cross slice eggs on egg slicer. 3. Combine mayonnaise, pickle relish, and salt. 4. Add dressing to eggs and mix gently. 5. Portion with No. 16 scoop. 6. Cut sandwiches in quarters or thirds for little fingers to handle.

TURKEY SALAD SANDWICH

INGREDIENTS	25 PORTIONS No. 20 Scoop	PORTIONS	PORTIONS	PROCEDURE
BONELESS TURKEY	6-1/2 cups (28 ounces)			1. Grind turkey or dice finely.
CELERY, diced	1 quart			2. Dice celery and add to turkey.
SALAD DRESSING	2 cups			3. Combine salad dressing, salt and turkey and mix.
SALT	1 tablespoon			4. Portion with No. 20 scoop per sandwich.
BREAD	50 slices			5. Cut sandwiches in quarters or thirds for little fingers to handle.
MARGARINE	1/2 pound			

TUNA FISH SALAD SANDWICH

INGREDIENTS	25 PORTIONS No. 20 Scoop	PORTIONS	PORTIONS	PROCEDURE
TUNA FISH	2 13 ounce cans			1. Drain tuna fish and separate into flakes.
CELERY, chopped	2-1/3 cups			2. Add chopped celery.
LEMON JUICE	1 tablespoon			3. Combine lemon juice, salt, pepper and salad dressing.
SALT	1/2 teaspoon			4. Add dressing to tuna fish and mix.
PEPPER	Dash			5. Portion with No. 20 scoop per sandwich.
SALAD DRESSING	1 cup			6. Cut sandwiches in quarters or thirds for little fingers to handle.
BREAD	50 slices			
MARGARINE	1/2 pound			

MEAT SALAD SANDWICH

INGREDIENTS	25 PORTIONS No. 20 Scoop	PORTIONS	PORTIONS	PROCEDURE
GROUND PORK, BEEF, OR HAM*	6 cups (25 ounces)			1. Add chopped celery to ground meat.
CELERY, chopped	1 cup			2. Combine relish, pepper, salt, and salad dressing.
SWEET PICKLE RELISH	3/4 cup			3. Mix dressing with meat and celery.
PEPPER	Dash			4. Portion with No. 20 scoop per sandwich.
SALT*	1 teaspoon			
SALAD DRESSING	1/2 cup			
BREAD	50 slices			
MARGARINE	1/2 pound			

*If ham is used—omit salt.

CHEESE SALAD SANDWICH

INGREDIENTS	25 PORTIONS	PORTIONS	PORTIONS	PROCEDURE
CHEESE (American or Cheddar)	1-1/2 pounds			1. Shred or grate cheese very finely.
SWEET PICKLES	1/4 cup			2. Finely chop pickles.
PIMIENTOS	1/4 cup			3. Finely chop pimiento.
SALAD DRESSING	3/4 cup			4. Mix cheese, pickles, pimiento, salad dressing and pickle juice until well blended.
SWEET PICKLE JUICE	3 tablespoons			5. Spread mixture on bread, close sandwiches. Use No. 20 scoop per sandwich.
MARGARINE *OR* BUTTER	1/2 pound			6. Cut sandwiches in quarters or thirds for little fingers to handle.
BREAD	50 slices			

PEANUT BUTTER–CARROT SANDWICH

INGREDIENTS	25 PORTIONS	PORTIONS	PORTIONS	PROCEDURE
CARROTS, grated	2 cups			1. Combine carrots, peanut butter, and marmalade. (May be mixed by hand or in mixer at slow speed.)
PEANUT BUTTER	1 pint			2. Spread bread with softened margarine or butter.
ORANGE MARMALADE	1 cup			3. Spread mixture on bread, close sandwiches. Use No. 20 scoop per sandwich.
MARGARINE *OR* BUTTER	1/2 pound			4. Cut sandwiches in quarters or thirds for little fingers to handle.
BREAD (Raisin or Whole Wheat is good)	50 slices			

TUNA BOAT SANDWICHES

Preheat oven to 200°F.

INGREDIENTS	25 PORTIONS	PORTIONS	PORTIONS	PROCEDURE
TUNA FISH, flaked	3 small cans or 18 to 21 ounces			1. Combine all ingredients 2. Fill each frankfurter bun with a No. 20 scoop rounded. 3. Place sandwiches on a baking sheet and heat for 30 minutes at 200°F.
HARD COOKED EGGS, chopped	6 each			
GREEN PEPPER, chopped	1/4 cup			
ONION, chopped	1/4 cup			
MAYONNAISE	1 cup			
CHEESE, CHEDDAR, chopped	1 cup (4 ounces)			
FRANKFURTER BUNS, (split)	25			

INGREDIENTS	PORTIONS	PORTIONS	PORTIONS	PROCEDURE

INGREDIENTS	PORTIONS	PORTIONS	PORTIONS	PROCEDURE

INGREDIENTS	PORTIONS	PORTIONS	PORTIONS	PROCEDURE

Vegetables

FROZEN VEGETABLES

FROZEN VEGETABLE	Weight Package	Water	Salt	Cooking Time After Return to Boil	Margarine	No. of Portions	Size Portion
Asparagus Cuts and Tips	2-1/2 lb.	1 qt.	1-1/2 tsp.	4-6 min.	2 oz.	16	2 oz.
Baby Green Lima Beans	2-1/2 lb.	1-1/2 qt.	1-1/2 tsp.	8-9 min.	2 oz.	21	2 oz.
Fordhook Lima Beans	2-1/2 lb.	1-1/2 qt.	1-1/2 tsp.	8-9 min.	2 oz.	20	2 oz.
Cut Green Beans	2-1/2 lb.	1 qt.	1-1/2 tsp.	5-6 min.	2 oz.	22	2 oz.
French Cut Green Beans	2-1/2 lb.	1 qt.	1-1/2 tsp.	5-6 min.	2 oz.	22	2 oz.
Cut Italian Green Beans	2-1/2 lb.	1 qt.	1-1/2 tsp.	5-6 min.	2 oz.	20	2 oz.
Cut Wax Beans	2-1/2 lb.	1 qt.	1-1/2 tsp.	5-6 min.	2 oz.	22	2 oz.
Broccoli	2 lb.	1 qt.	1-1/2 tsp.	6-7 min.	2 oz.	13	2 oz.
Brussels Sprouts	2 to 2-1/2 lb.	1 qt.	1-1/2 tsp.	7 min.	2 oz.	16-18	2 oz.
Cauliflower	2 lb.	3/4 qt.	1-1/2 tsp.	2-3 min.	2 oz.	16	2 oz.
Cut Corn	2-1/2 lb.	3/4 qt.	1-1/2 tsp.	3 min.	2 oz.	22	2 oz.
Peas	2-1/2 lb.	3/4 qt.	1 tbsp. sugar 1-1/2 tsp. salt	4-5 min.	2 oz.	22	2 oz.
Leaf Spinach (defrost partially and cut blocks into 8ths.)	3 lb.	1 qt.	1-1/2 tsp.	4-5 min.	2 oz.	20	2 oz.
Turnip Greens with Turnips (defrost partially and cut blocks into 8ths.)	3 lb.	1 qt.	1-1/2 tsp.	5 min.	Bacon fat	21	2 oz.

GENERAL PROCEDURE

1. Bring water to boiling in steam jacketed kettle or in pot or pan on top of range.
2. Add salt. Plunge frozen vegetable in. (Do *not* thaw any vegetable first.) Return quickly to a gentle boil. Time from this point. Break clusters of vegetable apart, if necessary. Stir gently once or twice to cook all pieces evenly.
3. When just crisply tender, put into serving pan with 1/4-inch to 1/2-inch vegetable liquid. (Save any extra liquid for use in soups, gravies, sauces.) Sprinkle melted clear fat over or proceed further with sauce as per menu.

SCALLOPED TOMATOES AND CELERY

Preheat oven to 375°F.

INGREDIENTS	25 PORTIONS 2 + ounces	PORTIONS	PORTIONS	PROCEDURE
CELERY, diced	3/4 quart			1. Steam celery until tender.
TOMATOES	1-1/2 quarts (6 No.303 cans)			2. Mix tomatoes with onions, tapioca, sugar and salt.
ONION, chopped finely	2 tablespoons			3. Pour 1/2 of tomato mixture into baking pan. Cover with celery–add remaining tomatoes.
TAPIOCA, INSTANT	2 tablespoons			4. Sprinkle with bread crumbs and margarine.
SUGAR	1/4 cup			5. Bake at 375°F. for 30 minutes.
SALT	2 teaspoons			
BREAD CRUMBS	1/2 cup			
MARGARINE, melted	1/4 cup			

BAKED ACORN SQUASH

Preheat oven to 375°F.

INGREDIENTS	27 PORTIONS 1/3's	PORTIONS	PORTIONS	PROCEDURE
SQUASH, ACORN, MEDIUM	9 each			1. Wash squash. Cut in 1/3's. Remove seeds.
MARGARINE	1/2 cup			2. Place squash upside down in shallow pan with 1/4-inch of water. Bake until tender at 375°F.–about 30 minutes.
SALT	1-1/2 teaspoons			3. When tender, place hollow side up.
BROWN SUGAR	1-3/4 cups			4. Melt margarine and pour over squash.
				5. Mix salt with brown sugar and place 1 tablespoon in each piece of squash.
				6. Bake at 350°F. for another 30 minutes.
VARIATION	*ADD*			*VARIATION*
APPLESAUCE	1-1/2 cups			1. Place 1 tablespoon of applesauce in each piece of squash and reduce sugar to 2 teaspoons per piece of squash.

CORN PUDDING

Preheat oven to 325°F.

INGREDIENTS	25 PORTIONS	PORTIONS	PORTIONS	PROCEDURE
EGGS	8 each			1. Beat eggs until well blended.
MILK	2 quarts			2. Stir in milk. Add salt and pepper.
SALT	1 tablespoon			3. Mix flour with a little of the corn, then add remainder of corn.
PEPPER	Dash			4. Combine with milk and egg mixture.
FLOUR	1/2 cup			5. Pour in well-greased 10-inch by 10-inch by 2-inch baking pan. Set pan in water bath.
CORN, CREAM STYLE	4 12 oz. cans			6. Bake at 325°F. for about 1 hour. Knife inserted in center will come out clean when done.
				7. Cut in squares (5x5). Serve.

ORANGE BEETS

INGREDIENTS	25 PORTIONS 2 ounces	PORTIONS	PORTIONS	PROCEDURE
BEETS, sliced or diced	1 No. 10 can or 2 No. 5 cans or 4 No. 2-1/2 cans			1. Drain beets, reserving the juice.
SALT	1 tablespoon			2. Mix salt, cornstarch, and sugar.
CORNSTARCH	1/2 cup			3. Add orange juice. Mix until smooth. Add to the beet juice. Boil until liquid is clear and starchy taste is gone.
SUGAR	1 cup			4. Add beets. Reheat.
ORANGE JUICE	1/2 cup			5. Portion with No. 10 scoop. Garnish with orange slices.
BEET JUICE AND WATER				
ORANGES				

CAULIFLOWER AU GRATIN

INGREDIENTS	25 PORTIONS 2 ounces	PORTIONS	PORTIONS	PROCEDURE
CAULIFLOWER, FLOWERETS	4 pounds			1. Remove outer leaves and stalks. Break cauliflower into flowerets. 2. Wash. Soak in salted water. Drain
BOILING WATER) LEMON JUICE) SALT)	2 quarts 1 tablespoon 1 tablespoon			3. Drop flowerets into boiling salted water. Cook until just tender, about 15 minutes. Drain.
CHEDDAR CHEESE, grated	8 ounces			4. Heat milk to scalding in double boiler or trunnion kettle. 5. Melt the margarine at low temperature and stir in the flour. Cook slowly about 5 minutes. DO NOT BROWN. 6. Slowly add milk (stirring) keeping sauce smooth. 7. Return cream sauce to kettle. Add grated cheese. 8. Add salt, pepper, and cooked cauliflower. Reheat. 9. Serve. Garnish with paprika.

MASHED HUBBARD SQUASH

Preheat oven to 350°F.

INGREDIENTS	25 PORTIONS 2 ounces	PORTIONS	PORTIONS	PROCEDURE
HUBBARD SQUASH, FROZEN, mashed MARGARINE SALT SUGAR	3-1/2 pounds (7 8 oz. pkgs.) 3 tablespoons 1 tablespoon 2 tablespoons			1. Put blocks of frozen squash into baking pan—1 layer deep, and defrost in 350°F. oven. 2. Blend margarine, salt, and sugar with squash. 3. Serve.

BRAISED CARROTS

Preheat oven to 450°F.

INGREDIENTS	25 PORTIONS 2 ounces	PORTIONS	PORTIONS	PROCEDURE
FRESH CARROTS	7 pounds			1. Wash, peel, and slice carrots 1/4 inch thick.
MARGARINE, melted	2 tablespoons			2. Cook carrots until tender. Drain.
SALT	2 teaspoons			3. Transfer to baking pan which has melted margarine in bottom.
SUGAR	2 tablespoons			4. Sprinkle salt and sugar over top of carrots. Mix gently.
MARGARINE, melted	2 tablespoons			5. Add second amount of melted margarine and place in 450°F. oven for about 10 to 12 minutes or until carrots are lightly brown on top and tender.

HARVARD BEETS

INGREDIENTS	25 PORTIONS 2+ ounces	PORTIONS	PORTIONS	PROCEDURE
BEETS, CANNED	1/2 No. 10 can or 2 No. 2-1/2 cans			1. Drain beets, save juice. 2. Heat juices to boiling. 3. Meanwhile mix sugar, cornstarch, salt, pepper, cloves and vinegar. Add to hot juice and cook until thick and clear—STIRRING WITH WIRE WHIP. 4. Remove from heat. Add margarine and coloring. 5. Add sauce to pre-heated beets; serve.
BEET JUICE (approx.)	1 pint +			
SUGAR	1/3 cup			
CORNSTARCH	1/3 cup			
SALT	1 teaspoon			
PEPPER	1/4 teaspoon			
CLOVES, ground	Dash			
VINEGAR	1/2 cup			
MARGARINE	2 tablespoons			
RED FOOD COLORING	1/4 teaspoon			

STEWED TOMATOES

INGREDIENTS	25 PORTIONS 2+ ounces	PORTIONS	PORTIONS	PROCEDURE
ONION, finely chopped	2 teaspoons			1. Cook onion in margarine.
MARGARINE	2 tablespoons			2. Add juice from tomatoes.
TOMATOES, CANNED	1/2 No. 10 can or 2 No. 2-1/2 cans			3. Add sugar and salt and bring to boil.
SUGAR	2 tablespoons			4. Add tomatoes and heat to serving temperature (160°F.).
SALT	1 teaspoon			

MEXICAN CORN

INGREDIENTS	25 PORTIONS 2+ ounces	PORTIONS	PORTIONS	PROCEDURE
ONION, chopped	1/2 cup			1. Saute chopped onion in margarine.
MARGARINE	2 tablespoons			2. Add green pepper and cook until onions are transparent.
GREEN PEPPER, chopped	1 small			3. Combine salt, sugar, and pepper. Dissolve in part of the liquid from the corn.
SALT	1 teaspoon			4. Add sauteed onion and pepper, seasonings and pimientos to corn.
SUGAR	1 teaspoon			5. Heat to boiling point and remove from fire.
WHITE PEPPER	Dash			6. Serve.
CORN, WHOLE KERNEL, CANNED	4 No. 303 cans or 8 cups			
PIMIENTOS, chopped	2 tablespoons			

BOILED BUTTER BEANS WITH HAM PIECES

INGREDIENTS	25 PORTIONS 3 ounces	PORTIONS	PORTIONS	PROCEDURE
DRY LIMA BEANS	2 pounds			1. Soak lima beans in cold water overnight.
SUGAR	3 tablespoons			2. Drain beans.
SALT	1/2 tablespoon			3. Add hot water, seasonings, onions and ham.
DRY MUSTARD	1 teaspoon			4. Cook until beans are tender, about 1 hour and 45 minutes.
HAM SHANK *OR* PIECES	2 pounds			
ONION, chopped	1/4 cup			
HOT WATER	1 quart + 1 cup			

BOSTON BAKED BEANS

Preheat oven to 300°F.

INGREDIENTS	25 PORTIONS 2 ounces	PORTIONS	PORTIONS	PROCEDURE
DRIED NAVY BEANS	2 pounds			1. Bake these beans the day before they are to be served.
WATER	To cover			2. Sort beans, removing imperfect beans and stones, wash, drain, wash, drain.
WATER	1 quart			3. Cover beans with water, bring to boil, drain.
SALT PORK, diced	12 ounces			4. Add measured water to beans—bring to boil. Transfer to heavy baking container, having cover to fit.
ONIONS, chopped	1 cup			
SALT	2 teaspoons			5. Add salt pork, onion, salt, dry mustard, black pepper, molasses and brown sugar. Mix. Cover and bake at 300°F. for 3 hours, add next amount of water periodically to keep water almost to level of beans.
DRY MUSTARD	2 teaspoons			
BLACK PEPPER	1/2 teaspoon			
MOLASSES, DARK	1/2 cup			
BROWN SUGAR	1/4 cup			
WATER	2-1/2 to 3 cups			6. Remove cover. Stir. Bake 2 to 3 hours more until beans are brown, still firm but done, and liquid is almost gone.
VINEGAR	2 tablespoons			7. Add vinegar and stir.

HOMEMADE BEANS IN TOMATO SAUCE

INGREDIENTS	25 PORTIONS 2 ounces	PORTIONS	PORTIONS	PROCEDURE
NAVY BEANS, DRIED	12 ounces			1. Pick over beans, wash, drain, wash, drain.
WATER	1 quart			2. Combine beans and water, and seasonings.
CATSUP	1/2 cup			3. Saute chopped onions in ground salt pork until onions are transparent.
MOLASSES, DARK	2 tablespoons			4. Add tomatoes to onions and bring to boil.
SALT	1 teaspoon			5. Add tomatoes to beans and simmer covered for approximately 2 hours or until beans are tender.
MONOSODIUM GLUTAMATE	1/2 teaspoon			6. If beans become too thick add extra water.
WORCESTERSHIRE SAUCE	1 teaspoon			
NUTMEG, GROUND	Dash			
CLOVES, GROUND	Dash			
MUSTARD, DRY	1/2 teaspoon			
ONION, chopped	1/4 cup			
SALT PORK, ground or chopped finely	2 ounces			
TOMATOES	1 cup			

SCALLOPED POTATOES

Preheat oven to 375°F.

INGREDIENTS	25 PORTIONS 2 ounces	PORTIONS	PORTIONS	PROCEDURE
SLICED RAW POTATOES	3 pounds			1. Wash, peel potatoes.
FLOUR	2 tablespoons			2. Slice potatoes 1/4 inch thick, blanch in steamer, or parboil until tender.
COLD MILK	2 tablespoons			3. Drain and place potatoes in greased baking pan.
LUKEWARM MILK	1 pint			4. Make paste of cold milk and flour.
SALT	1-1/2 teaspoons			5. Stir paste, salt, pepper, and onion in warm milk.
WHITE PEPPER	1/4 teaspoon			6. Pour milk mixture over potatoes.
MINCED RAW ONION	1 tablespoon			7. Pour melted margarine over potatoes.
MARGARINE, melted	2 tablespoons			8. Bake at 375°F. for 45 to 50 minutes.

MASHED POTATOES

INGREDIENTS	25 PORTIONS 2 ounces	PORTIONS	PORTIONS	PROCEDURE
RAW POTATOES DRY MILK POWDER SALT WHITE PEPPER MARGARINE *OR* BUTTER, melted HOT WATER	4 pounds 3 cups 1 tablespoon 1/8 teaspoon 2 tablespoons 2 quarts (approx.)			1. Wash, peel, and cut potatoes in quarters. Cook until tender. 2. Drain, place in mixing bowl and sprinkle dry milk powder, salt, and pepper over top of potatoes. 3. Beat with wire whip until potatoes are completely broken up. Add melted margarine. 4. Slowly add hot water to desired consistency. 5. Beat until light and fluffy.

TOMATO HALVES WITH CHEESE

Preheat oven to 400°F.

INGREDIENTS	25 PORTIONS	PORTIONS	PORTIONS	PROCEDURE
TOMATOES, medium size, ripe	13 each			1. Rinse, dry, and cut tomatoes in half crosswise.
MARGARINE	1/2 cup			2. Place tomatoes, cut side up on bun pan.
PREPARED MUSTARD	1 tablespoon			3. Combine margarine, bread crumbs, grated cheese, salt and mustard.
DRY BREAD CRUMBS	1 cup			4. Sprinkle crumb mixture over tomatoes.
SALT	1 teaspoon			5. Bake at 400°F. for 20 to 25 minutes.
CHEDDAR CHEESE	2 ounces, grated			

SWEET POTATO PUFFS

Preheat oven to 350°F.

INGREDIENTS	25 PORTIONS 2 ounces No. 20 Scoop	PORTIONS	PORTIONS	PROCEDURE
SWEET POTATOES, canned MARGARINE *OR* BUTTER SUGAR, GRANULATED LIGHT BROWN SUGAR SALT CINNAMON COCONUT, shredded	2 No. 2-1/2 cans 1/4 cup 1/4 cup 2 tablespoons 2 teaspoons 1 teaspoon 2 cups (6 ounces)			1. Heat sweet potatoes and liquid. 2. Mash sweet potatoes in mixer. Add margarine, granulated sugar, light brown sugar, salt, cinnamon. 3. Portion with No. 20 scoop. Form into round flat patties. 4. Roll in coconut. 5. Place greased brown paper on sheet pan. 6. Bake in oven at 350°F. for approximately 20 minutes.

CAULIFLOWER AU GRATIN

Preheat oven to 350°F.

INGREDIENTS	25 PORTIONS 2 ounces	PORTIONS	PORTIONS	PROCEDURE
CAULIFLOWER, FRESH *OR* CAULIFLOWER, FROZEN	2 large heads (3 to 4 lbs.) 1 2-1/2 pound box			1. Clean and trim cauliflower; soak in salt water for 30 minutes. Rinse and drain. 2. Separate cauliflower into flowerets. 3. Place cauliflower in rapidly boiling salted water and cook until tender. Drain. 4. Place cauliflower in buttered baking pan. 5. Cover with cheese sauce. 6. Combine bread crumbs and paprika and sprinkle over sauce. Drizzle with melted margarine. 7. Bake at 350°F. for 20 minutes.
CHEESE SOUP	2 10-1/2 ounce cans			
BREAD CRUMBS	1/4 cup			
PAPRIKA	1/4 teaspoon			
MARGARINE, melted	2 tablespoons			

SPINACH CUSTARD

Preheat oven to 350°F.

INGREDIENTS	25 PORTIONS 2 ounces	PORTIONS	PORTIONS	PROCEDURE
FROZEN CHOPPED SPINACH	3 10 ounce packages			1. Thaw and drain spinach.
MILK	3 cups			2. Grease baking ban–prepare water bath.
EGGS, LARGE (beaten lightly)	9 each			3. Combine spinach, milk, eggs, vinegar, salt and pepper with a fork until well blended.
VINEGAR	3 tablespoons			4. Pour into greased baking pan (12-inch by 12-inch by 2-inch).
SALT	1 tablespoon			5. Bake in water bath at 350°F. for 60 minutes–or until knife comes out clean.
PEPPER	Dash			6. Cut in portions (5 x 5).

MARINATED CARROTS

Prepare day before serving

INGREDIENTS	25 PORTIONS 2 ounces +	PORTIONS	PORTIONS	PROCEDURE
SLICED CARROTS, cooked or canned	6 cups or 3 No. 303 cans			1. Mix vinegar, oil, sugar, salt and pepper.
GREEN PEPPER, finely chopped	1 cup			2. Drain carrots—mix with pepper, pimiento, green onions and celery. Toss lightly.
PIMIENTO, chopped	1 3 ounce jar			3. Add vegetables to vinegar and oil mixture.
GREEN ONIONS, chopped	1 small bunch			4. Chill about 24 hours and serve.
CELERY, chopped	1 cup			
VINEGAR	2 cups			
SALAD OIL	1 cup			
SUGAR	2-1/4 cups			
SALT	2 teaspoons			
PEPPER	1 teaspoon			

INGREDIENTS	PORTIONS	PORTIONS	PORTIONS	PROCEDURE

INGREDIENTS	PORTIONS	PORTIONS	PORTIONS	PROCEDURE

INGREDIENTS	PORTIONS	PORTIONS	PORTIONS	PROCEDURE

JELLIED CARROT AND PINEAPPLE SALAD

INGREDIENTS	25 PORTIONS 12- x 12- x 2-in. pan	PORTIONS	PORTIONS	PROCEDURE
LEMON GELATIN	1 cup (6 ounce)			1. Dissolve gelatin and salt in hot liquid.
SALT	1-1/4 teaspoons			
BOILING WATER	3-1/2 cups			
LEMON JUICE	1 tablespoon			2. Add lemon juice and chill until slightly thickened.
CARROTS, grated	2 cups			3. Combine grated carrots and drained crushed pineapple and fold into slightly thickened gelatin.
CRUSHED PINEAPPLE, drained	1 cup			4. Chill until firm in 12-inch by 12-inch by 2-inch pan.
				5. Cut in squares (5 x 5). Serve.

KIDNEY BEAN SALAD

INGREDIENTS	25 PORTIONS 2 ounces	PORTIONS	PORTIONS	PROCEDURE
KIDNEY BEANS, CANNED, drained	1 No. 5 can or 2 No. 2-1/2 cans or 7 cups			1. Drain kidney beans.
EGGS, hard-cooked, finely chopped	5 each			2. Add chopped eggs to kidney beans.
MAYONNAISE	1/2 cup			3. Pour dressing over beans and eggs.
SWEET PICKLE RELISH	1/2 cup			4. Add rest of ingredients.
CELERY, diced finely	2-1/2 cups			5. Mix gently to avoid crushing eggs.
ONION, chopped finely	3 tablespoons			
SALT	1 teaspoon			
PEPPER	1/8 teaspoon			

PICKLED BEETS AND ONION SALAD

INGREDIENTS	25 PORTIONS Approx. 2 ounces	PORTIONS	PORTIONS	PROCEDURE
CANNED BEETS, drained	1-1/2 quarts			1. Drain beet slices and cut into 1/2 inch cubes.
ONION, chopped	1/2 cup			2. Slice onion 1/4 inch thick and dice.
VINEGAR	6 tablespoons			3. Combine vinegar, salad oil, sugar and salt.
SALAD OIL	3 tablespoons			4. Pour dressing over beets and onoins.
SUGAR	1/2 tablespoon			5. Allow to stand at least for 1/2 hour before portioning.
SALT	1 teaspoon			6. Portion with No. 20 scoop.

POTATO SALAD

INGREDIENTS	25 PORTIONS 2 ounces	PORTIONS	PORTIONS	PROCEDURE
POTATOES, cooked, peeled and diced in 1/2 inch cubes	1-1/2 pounds			1. Combine salad oil and vinegar and pour over diced potatoes; toss and allow to set 15 minutes. 2. Add eggs, celery, green pepper, pimiento, and parsley. Toss lightly to avoid breaking potatoes and eggs. 3. Blend mayonnaise, salad dressing, onion, prepared mustard, salt and green pepper. Add to potato mixture and mix gently. 4. Allow to refrigerate at least 1/2 hour before portioning. 5. Portion with No. 20 scoop
SALAD OIL	2 tablespoons			
VINEGAR	1 tablespoon			
EGGS, hard-cooked, quartered and diced	4 each			
CELERY, diced	1 cup			
GREEN PEPPER, diced	1/2 cup			
PIMIENTO, diced	2 tablespoons			
PARSLEY, chopped	1 tablespoon			
MAYONNAISE	1/2 cup			
SALAD DRESSING	1/2 cup			
ONION, grated, including juice	2-1/4 teaspoons			
PREPARED MUSTARD	2-1/4 teaspoons			
SALT	2-1/4 teaspoons			
WHITE PEPPER	1/4 teaspoon			

TOSSED VEGETABLE SALAD

INGREDIENTS	25 PORTIONS 1-1/2 ounces	PORTIONS	PORTIONS	PROCEDURE
HEAD LETTUCE (48'S)	1 large head (10 ounces)			1. Wash greens and drain. 2. Cut head lettuce, leaf lettuce, escarole and endive into 1/2 inch pieces. 3. Slice carrots and unpeeled cucumbers thin and add to greens along with sliced celery. 4. Add dressing of choice and toss slightly. 5. Garnish with tomato wedge.
Add 3 of the following:				
A. LEAF LETTUCE	1/2 bunch (6 oz.)			
B. ESCAROLE	1/2 bunch (6 oz.)			
C. ENDIVE	1/2 bunch (6 oz.)			
D. RED CABBAGE	6 ounces			
CUCUMBERS	1/2 medium			
CARROTS	1 medium			
CELERY, sliced	1/2 cup			
DRESSING	1/2 cup			
TOMATO	3 each medium			

CARROT AND RAISIN SALAD

INGREDIENTS	25 PORTIONS No. 20 Scoop	PORTIONS	PORTIONS	PROCEDURE
RAISINS	1-1/4 cups			1. Combine raisins, water, sugar, salt, and lemon juice in sauce pan, cover and simmer for 5 minutes.
WATER	2 cups			2. Remove from heat–let stand until raisins are plump. Drain and cool.
SUGAR	1-1/2 teaspoons			3. Wash, scrape and shred carrots.
SALT	Dash			4. Combine carrots, salad dressing, and raisins.
LEMON JUICE	2 teaspoons			5. Portion with No. 20 scoop.
CARROTS, RAW, shredded	2 pounds			
SALAD DRESSING	1 cup			

VITAMIN SALAD

INGREDIENTS	25 PORTIONS 12- x 12- x 2-in. pan	PORTIONS	PORTIONS	PROCEDURE
LEMON GELATIN	1 cup (6 ounce)			1. Dissolve gelatin and salt in hot water.
SALT	1 teaspoon			2. Add ice covered with juice and water.
BOILING WATER	2 cups			3. Add vinegar.
ICE covered with juice and water	1-3/4 cups			4. Chill until slightly thickened.
VINEGAR	1 tablespoon			5. Fold in pineapple, cabbage, apples, celery, green pepper, and carrots.
CRUSHED PINEAPPLE, drained	1/2 cup			6. Chill until firm in 12-inch by 12-inch by 2-inch pan.
CABBAGE, chopped	1/2 cup			7. Cut in squares (5 x 5). Serve.
APPLE, diced	1/2 cup			
CELERY, sliced	1/2 cup			
GREEN PEPPER, chopped	1/2 cup			
CARROT, shredded	1/2 cup			

SPINACH SALAD

INGREDIENTS	25 PORTIONS	PORTIONS	PORTIONS	PROCEDURE
RAW SPINACH	1 cello package (1 pound)			1. Wash spinach thoroughly and trim split ends and leaves. Drain.
VINEGAR	1 tablespoon			2. Chop coarsely.
SALT	1/2 tablespoon			3. Combine vinegar, salt, sour cream and mayonnaise.
SOUR CREAM	1 cup (8 ounces)			4. Add dressing to spinach. Drain well.
MAYONNAISE*	1/4 cup			5. Portion and garnish with chopped egg.
EGGS, hard-cooked, chopped	5 each			
*Salad dressing or a vinegar and oil dressing may be used for variety.				

STUFFED CELERY SALAD–CHEESE OR PEANUT BUTTER

INGREDIENTS	25 PORTIONS 2-3 inch stalks	PORTIONS	PORTIONS	PROCEDURE
CELERY STALKS	50 stalks (1 large bunch)			1. Clean and trim celery stalks. Cut in 3 inch lengths and approximately 3/4 to 1 inch wide.
CREAM CHEESE	6 ounces			2. Blend cream cheese, mayonnaise, and milk.
MAYONNAISE	1/4 cup			3. Fill celery stalks with cheese mixture.
MILK	1/4 cup			4. Garnish with light sprinkle of paprika for color interest.
PAPRIKA				5. Portion 2 stalks per serving.
PEANUT BUTTER FILLING				
PEANUT BUTTER, SMOOTH STYLE	3/4 cup (6 ounces)			
HONEY	1/4 cup			
FRUIT JUICE	1/4 cup			

COMPLEXION SALAD

INGREDIENTS	25 PORTIONS 2 ounces	PORTIONS	PORTIONS	PROCEDURE
CARROTS, edible portion	2 pounds			1. Chop or grate carrots and cabbage very fine.
CABBAGE, edible portion	4 ounces			2. Combine mayonnaise, raisins, brown sugar, and salt.
MAYONNAISE	1/2 cup			3. Pour dressing over cabbage and carrots and mix well.
RAISINS	1/2 cup			4. Portion using No. 20 scoop.
BROWN SUGAR	2 tablespoons			5. Garnish with tomato wedge.
SALT	1/2 teaspoon			
TOMATOES	3 each			

INGREDIENTS	PORTIONS	PORTIONS	PORTIONS	PROCEDURE

INGREDIENTS	PORTIONS	PORTIONS	PORTIONS	PROCEDURE

VEGETABLE SALAD

INGREDIENTS	PORTIONS	PORTIONS	PORTIONS	PROCEDURE

RAW FRUITS AND VEGETABLES–SNACKS

Some of the fruits and vegetables listed may be eaten raw. Wedges, leaves, or pieces may take the place of a salad. These should be thoroughly washed. To be palatable, vegetables must be clean and crisp. They may be crisped in the hydrator of an automatic refrigerator or wrapped in a damp, clean cloth and placed in the ice box. Fruits with tough skins should be peeled for easier chewing.

FRUIT OR VEGETABLE	25 PORTIONS	NOTES
APPLE OR PEAR WEDGE	1-1/2 pounds	Cut into 1-inch wedges just before serving.
APRICOT HALVES	2 pounds	Cut in halves. Remove stones.
CABBAGE WEDGES	2 pounds	Cut in 1/2 inch wedges. Chop for younger children.
CARROT STICKS	1-1/2 pounds	Select young carrots. Cut into 2-inch lengths and then in thin strips.
CELERY STICKS	1 large bunch	Remove tough strings. Cut into 2-inch pieces.
LETTUCE–HEAD	1 large head	Cut out core. Separate leaves breaking large ones in half.
LETTUCE–LEAF	1-1/2 pounds	Separate leaves and remove ends.
ORANGE OR TANGERINE WEDGES	1-1/2 pounds	Wash and remove skins. Separate into sections.
PEACH WEDGES	2 pounds	Scald peaches, dip in cold water. Peel. Cut in halves, remove stones. Cut in wedges.
SPINACH LEAVES	1 pound	Separate leaves and remove ends.
TOMATO WEDGES	2 pounds	Remove stem. Cut in wedges.
TURNIP STICKS	1-1/2 pounds	Cut into 1/2 inch slices. Pare and cut slices into strips.

VEGETABLE SNACK

INGREDIENTS	PORTIONS	PORTIONS	PORTIONS	PROCEDURE

INGREDIENTS	PORTIONS	PORTIONS	PORTIONS	PROCEDURE

VEGETABLE SNACK

VEGETABLE SNACK

INGREDIENTS	PORTIONS	PORTIONS	PORTIONS	PROCEDURE

Fruits

CANNED FRUIT–SERVINGS PER CAN

FRUIT	SIZE OF CAN	PORTIONS	PORTION SIZE	CAN COUNT OR WEIGHT
Applesauce	1 No. 303	4	4 ounces	1 pound
Applesauce	1 No. 10	25	4 ounces	6 lb. 13 oz.
Apricots	1 No. 2-1/2	5	4 halves	18/20 count
Apricots	1 No. 10	22	4 halves	83/108 count
Figs	1 No. 2-1/2	9	3 Figs	27 count
Figs	1 No. 10	33	3 Figs	90/110 count
Fruit Cocktail	1 No. 2-1/2	5	5 ounces	1 lb. 13 oz.
Fruit Cocktail	1 No. 10	20	5 ounces	6 lb. 12 oz.
Peach Halves	1 No. 2-1/2	5	2 halves	1 lb. 13 oz.
Peach Halves	1 No. 10	18/20	2 halves	35/40 count
Peach Slices	1 No. 2-1/2	5	4 ounces	1 lb. 13 oz.
Peach Slices	1 No. 10	25	4 ounces	6 lb. 12 oz.
Pear Halves	1 No. 2-1/2	5	2 halves	1 lb. 13 oz.
Pear Halves	1 No. 10	18/20	2 halves	35/40 count
Pineapple Chunks	1 No. 2	4	1/2 cup	1 lb. 4-1/2 oz.
Pineapple Chunks	1 No. 10	25	1/2 cup	6 lb. 13 oz.
Pineapple Slices	1 No. 2	5	2 slices	10 slices
Pineapple Slices	1 No. 10	26	2 slices	52 count
Prunes	1 lb. jar	4-1/2	4 Prunes	18 count
Prunes	1 No. 10	28	4 Prunes	140 count
Royal Anne Cherries	1 lb. jar	4-1/3	12 Cherries	52 count
Royal Anne Cherries	1 No. 10	22	12 Cherries	6 lb. 12 oz.

FRESH FRUIT CUP

INGREDIENTS	25 PORTIONS	PORTIONS	PORTIONS	PROCEDURE
ORANGES, LARGE (48 size)	4 each			1. Peel and section oranges. Cut sections in half.
BANANAS	2 pounds			2. Peel bananas and slice—cover with orange juice to keep from turning dark.
APPLES	2 pounds			3. Wash, core and dice apples. Mix with bananas and oranges.
SEEDLESS GRAPES	1/2 pound			4. Wash grapes and cut in half. Mix all fruits. Chill.
				5. Portion with No. 20 scoop.

FRIED APPLE SLICES

Preheat oven to 375°F.

INGREDIENTS	25 PORTIONS 2 ounces	PORTIONS	PORTIONS	PROCEDURE
APPLES, sliced, unpared	4 pounds			1. Saute apples in hot fat until almost tender, about 30 minutes.
MARGARINE *OR* BACON FAT	3/4 cup			2. Add sugar and salt. Cook until tender or finish in oven at 375°F.
SUGAR	3/4 cup			3. Portion with No. 10 scoop.
SALT	1 teaspoon			

STEWED APRICOTS

INGREDIENTS	25 PORTIONS 4 halves	PORTIONS	PORTIONS	PROCEDURE
APRICOTS, DRIED	2-1/2 pounds			1. Wash apricots thoroughly.
COLD WATER	2 quarts			2. Cover apricots with cold water and add sugar and lemon juice.
SUGAR	2 cups			3. Bring to a boil. Remove from heat. Cool in apricot liquor.
LEMON JUICE	1 tablespoon			

BAKED APPLES

Preheat oven to 350°F.

INGREDIENTS	25 PORTIONS 1 each	PORTIONS	PORTIONS	PROCEDURE
BAKING APPLES Roman Beauty or Stayman 100-120 count	25 each			1. Wash and core apples. Peel a ring from top of apple. 2. Place in baking pan, peeled side down.
CINNAMON IMPERIALS	1/2 cup (4 ounce)			3. Add water and cinnamon imperials.
WATER	1 quart			4. Cover with lid or foil and bake at 350°F. for 40 minutes.
SUGAR	1 quart + 1/2 cup			5. Uncover, turn apples over (peeled side up). Sprinkle sugar over top of apples. Add 1/4 teaspoon of melted margarine per apple.
MARGARINE, melted	2 tablespoons + 1/4 teaspoon			6. Continue baking until apples are tender. Baste frequently with cinnamon syrup.

STEWED OR BAKED RHUBARB

Preheat oven to 350°F.

INGREDIENTS	25 PORTIONS	PORTIONS	PORTIONS	PROCEDURE
RHUBARB, FRESH SUGAR WATER	4 pounds 2 cups 1 cup			1. Remove root end and leaves from stalks of rhubarb. WASH. Cut into 1 inch pieces. 2. Place rhubarb into baking pan. Sprinkle with sugar and add water. Stir. 3. Cover. Bake at 350°F. until tender (about 1-1/2 hours). Do not stir. Cool and serve.

INGREDIENTS	PORTIONS	PORTIONS	PORTIONS	PROCEDURE

INGREDIENTS	PORTIONS	PORTIONS	PORTIONS	PROCEDURE

INGREDIENTS	PORTIONS	PORTIONS	PORTIONS	PROCEDURE

JELLIED ORANGE OR ORANGE-GRAPEFRUIT AMBROSIA SALAD

INGREDIENTS	25 PORTIONS 12- x 12-x 2-in. pan	PORTIONS	PORTIONS	PROCEDURE
ORANGES, sectioned or sliced and diced	1-1/2 cups			1. Drain oranges, reserving juice.
ORANGE GELATIN	1 cup (6 ounces)			2. Dissolve gelatin and salt in boiling water.
SALT	1/4 teaspoon			3. Add ice covered with orange juice.
BOILING WATER	2 cups			4. Chill until slightly thickened.
ICE covered with orange juice	1-1/2 cups			5. Fold in oranges, orange rind, sliced bananas and coconut.
ORANGE RIND, grated	1/2 teaspoon			6. Chill until firm in 12-inch by 12-inch by 2-inch pan.
BANANAS, sliced	1-1/2 cups (2 each)			7. Cut in squares (5 x 5). Serve.
COCONUT	1/4 cup (3/4 ounce)			
FOR ORANGE-GRAPEFRUIT AMBROSIA, replace bananas with 1-1/2 cups grapefruit.				

JELLIED CITRUS RUBY SALAD

INGREDIENTS	25 PORTIONS 12- x 12- x 2-inch pan	PORTIONS	PORTIONS	PROCEDURE
STRAWBERRY *OR* RASPBERRY GELATIN	1 cup (6 ounces)			1. Dissolve gelatin in hot water.
BOILING WATER	2 cups			2. Drain citrus sections, and reserve juice.
ICE covered with water and citrus juice	1-3/4 cups			3. Add ice covered with water and citrus juice.
GRAPEFRUIT SECTIONS (cut in 1/2-inch pieces)	1 cup			4. Chill until slightly thickened.
ORANGE SECTIONS (cut in 1/2 inch pieces)	1 cup			5. Fold in citrus sections.
				6. Chill until firm in 12-inch by 12-inch by 2-inch pan.
				7. Cut in squares (5 x 5). Serve.

JELLIED FRUIT AND CREAM CHEESE SALAD

INGREDIENTS	25 PORTIONS 12- x 12- x 2-in. pan	PORTIONS	PORTIONS	PROCEDURE
CREAM CHEESE	3 ounces			1. Allow cream cheese to come to room temperature.
LEMON, LIME *OR* ORANGE GELATIN	1/2 cup (3 ounces)			2. Dissolve gelatin in hot water.
BOILING WATER	1-3/4 cups			3. Chill slightly but not enough to start congealing.
				4. Add softened cream cheese and blend thoroughly.
RED GELATIN	1/2 cup (3 ounces)			5. **While first** gelatin mixture is cooling, dissolve red gelatin in second measure of hot water.
BOILING WATER	1-1/2 cups			6. Add lemon juice.
LEMON JUICE	1 tablespoon			7. Chill until slightly thickened.
FRUIT COCKTAIL, drained	2 cups			8. Fold in fruit cocktail.
				9. Pour fruit cocktail gelatin in 12-inch by 12-inch by 2-inch pan.
				10. Top with cream cheese gelatin.
				11. Chill until firm.
				12. Cut in squares (5 x 5). Serve.

WALDORF SALAD

INGREDIENTS	25 PORTIONS 2 + ounces	PORTIONS	PORTIONS	PROCEDURE
EATING APPLES (see caramel apple recipe p. 160 for listing)	3 pounds			1. Wash apples. 2. Cut unpeeled apples into quarters and core. Cut each quarter into 3 or 4 slices. Cut slices into 3/8-inch wedges. Do not peel. Cut apples into lemon juice and water solution and leave for a couple of minutes. Drain.
CELERY, diced	3 cups			3. Add celery and mix.
MAYONNAISE	1 cup			4. Gently fold whipped topping, sugar into mayonnaise.
WHIPPED TOPPING	1/2 cup			5. Add dressing to apples and celery.
SUGAR	2 tablespoons			6. Use No. 20 scoop to portion.

FRESH FRUIT SALAD

INGREDIENTS	25 PORTIONS No. 20 Scoop	PORTIONS	PORTIONS	PROCEDURE
Use 1 or both of these: ORANGE SECTIONS *AND/OR* GRAPEFRUIT SECTIONS	 3 cups			1. Prepare fruit and mix. 2. Slice bananas and dip in pineapple or citrus juice. 3. Add bananas to fruit mix just befor serving.
Use 1 or both of these: PINEAPPLE TIDBITS *AND/OR* GRAPES, GREEN, SEEDLESS, halved	 1 cup			
Use 1 or more of these: APPLES, diced 1/2 inch PEARS, diced 1/2 inch MELON BALLS PEACHES, diced 1/2 inch	 1 cup			
BANANAS	2 each			

RABBIT SALAD

INGREDIENTS	25 PORTIONS	PORTIONS	PORTIONS	PROCEDURE
LETTUCE	1 large head			1. Wash, drain, and shred.
PEAR HALVES	1 No. 10 can			2. Arrange lettuce nests on individual plates.
MARSHMALLOWS	25 each (1 pound)			3. Drain pear halves.
OR CREAM CHEESE	6 ounces			4. Place drained pear half cut-side down on lettuce nest.
MARASCHINO CHERRIES	13 each			5. At larger end of pear place marshmallow for tail or a cream cheese ball.
RAISINS	50 each			6. Stem end of pear is the head, make mouth with 1/2 maraschino cherry—eyes with raisins.
ALMONDS	50 each			7. Two (2) almonds make large straight ears.

BANANA GELATIN SALAD

INGREDIENTS	25 PORTIONS 12- x 12- x 2-in. pan	PORTIONS	PORTIONS	PROCEDURE
RED RASPBERRY GELATIN	1 cup (6 ounces)			1. Dissolve gelatin in hot water.
BOILING WATER	2 cups			2. Add ice water to gelatin mixture.
ICE covered with water	2 cups			3. Chill until slightly thickened.
BANANAS, sliced	1 pound (as purchased)			4. Fold in bananas.
				5. Chill until firm in a 12-inch by 12-inch by 2-inch pan.
				6. Cut in squares (5 x 5). Garnish with whipped topping. Serve.

JELLIED FRUIT SALAD

INGREDIENTS	25 PORTIONS 12- x 12- x 2-in. pan	PORTIONS	PORTIONS	PROCEDURE
RED RASPBERRY GELATIN	1 cup (6 ounces)			1. Dissolve gelatin in boiling water.
BOILING WATER	2 cups			2. Add iced water.
ICE covered with fruit juice and water	1-1/2 cups			3. Chill until slightly thickened.
FRUIT COCKTAIL, drained	2 cups (No. 303 can or No. 2 can)			4. Fold in well-drained fruit and mix thoroughly.
				5. Chill until firm (12-inch by 12-inch by 2-inch pan).
				6. Cut in squares (5 x 5). Serve.

JELLIED PEACH SALAD

INGREDIENTS	25 PORTIONS 12- x 12- x 2-in. pan	PORTIONS	PORTIONS	PROCEDURE
ORANGE GELATIN	1 cup (6 ounces)			1. Dissolve gelatin in hot water.
HOT WATER	2 cups			2. Add iced juice and water.
ICED JUICE AND WATER	1-1/2 cups			3. Chill until slightly thickened.
PEACH SLICES, drained	2 cups			4. Fold in well-drained peaches and mix thoroughly.
				5. Chill until firm in 12-inch by 12-inch by 2-inch pan.
				6. Cut in squares (5 x 5). Serve.

JELLIED PEAR SALAD

INGREDIENTS	25 PORTIONS 12- x 12- x 2- in. pan	PORTIONS	PORTIONS	PROCEDURE
LIME GELATIN	1 cup (6 ounces)			1. Dissolve gelatin in hot water.
BOILING WATER	2 cups			2. Add iced juice and water.
ICED JUICE AND WATER	1-1/2 cups			3. Chill until slightly thickened.
PEARS, diced and drained	2 cups			4. Fold in well-drained pears and mix thoroughly.
				5. Chill until firm in 12-inch by 12-inch by 2-inch pan.
				6. Cut in squares (5 x 5). Serve.

JELLIED PEAR AND CHEESE SALAD

INGREDIENTS	25 PORTIONS 12- x 12- x 2-in. pan	PORTIONS	PORTIONS	PROCEDURE
LIME GELATIN	1 cup (6 ounces)			1. Dissolve gelatin and salt in hot liquid.
SALT	1/4 teaspoon			2. Add vinegar.
BOILING WATER AND PEAR JUICE	3 cups			3. Pour half of mixture into 12-inch by 12-inch by 2-inch pan. Chill until firm.
VINEGAR	2 teaspoons			4. Chill remaining half of gelatin mixture until slightly thickened.
CREAM COTTAGE CHEESE	1 cup			5. Add ginger to cottage cheese.
GINGER, GROUND	1/4 teaspoon			6. Fold cottage cheese and pears into thickened gelatin.
CANNED PEARS, drained, diced	2 cups			7. Spread over firm gelatin, chill until firm.
				8. Cut into squares (5 x 5). Serve.

JELLIED PINEAPPLE STRAWBERRY SALAD

INGREDIENTS	25 PORTIONS 12- x 12- x 2-in. pan	PORTIONS	PORTIONS	PROCEDURE
STRAWBERRY GELATIN	1 cup (6 ounces)			1. Dissolve gelatin in hot water.
BOILING WATER	2 cups			2. Add ice covered with water and chill until slightly thickened.
ICE covered with juice and water	1-3/4 cups			3. Fold in pineapple.
CRUSHED PINEAPPLE, well drained	2 cups			4. Chill until firm in 12-inch by 12-inch by 2-inch pan.
				5. Cut in squares (5 x 5). Serve.

MOLDED GOLDEN GLOW SALAD

INGREDIENTS	25 PORTIONS 12- x 12- x 2-in. pan	PORTIONS	PORTIONS	PROCEDURE
ORANGE GELATIN	1 cup (6 ounces)			1. Dissolve gelatin and salt in hot liquid.
SALT	1-1/4 teaspoons			2. Add orange juice, and lemon juice.
BOILING WATER	2 cups			3. Chill until partially set and fold in chopped carrots, crushed pineapple, and diced celery.
ORANGE JUICE	1-1/2 cups			4. Chill until firm in 12-inch by 12-inch by 2-inch pan.
LEMON JUICE	1 tablespoon			5. Cut in squares (5 x 5). Serve.
CARROTS, finely chopped	1 cup			
CRUSHED PINEAPPLE drained	1 cup			
CELERY, finely diced	1 cup			

JELLIED CRANBERRY, APPLE AND NUT SALAD

INGREDIENTS	25 PORTIONS 12- x 12- x 2- in. pan	PORTIONS	PORTIONS	PROCEDURE
RED GELATIN (strawberry, cherry, or raspberry)	1 cup (6 ounces)			1. Dissolve gelatin and salt in hot water.
SALT	3/4 teaspoon			2. Add ice covered with water and lemon juice.
BOILING WATER	2 cups			3. Chill until slightly thickened.
ICE covered with water	1-1/2 cups			4. Fold in apples, pecans, and cranberry sauce.
LEMON JUICE	2 teaspoons			5. Chill until firm in 12-inch by 12-inch by 2-inch pan.
APPLE, unpeeled, diced	1/2 cup			6. Cut in squares (5 x 5). Serve.
PECANS, chopped	1/4 cup			
WHOLE CRANBERRY SAUCE, CANNED	2 cups			

JELLIED PEAR AND GRAPE SALAD

INGREDIENTS	25 PORTIONS 12- x 12- x 2-in. pan	PORTIONS	PORTIONS	PROCEDURE
CHERRY GELATIN	1 cup (6 ounces)			1. Dissolve gelatin in hot water.
BOILING WATER	2 cups			2. Add ice covered with juice and water.
ICE covered with pear juice and water	1-3/4 cups			3. Chill until slightly thickened.
GRAPES, halved and seeded	1 cup			4. Fold in grapes and pears.
PEARS, diced and drained	1-1/2 cups			5. Chill until firm in 12-inch by 12-inch by 2-inch pan.
				6. Cut in squares (5 x 5). Serve.

MOLDED BLACK CHERRY WALDORF SALAD

INGREDIENTS	25 PORTIONS 12- x 12- x 2-in. pan	PORTIONS	PORTIONS	PROCEDURE
BLACK CHERRY GELATIN	1 cup (6 ounces)			1. Dissolve gelatin in hot water. 2. Add ice covered with water. 3. Chill until slightly thickened. 4. Fold in fruit and nuts. 5. Chill until firm in 12-inch by 12-inch by 2-inch pan. 6. Cut in squares (5 x 5). Serve.
BOILING WATER	2 cups			
ICE covered with cold water	1-3/4 cups			
APPLES, peeled, diced	1-1/2 cups			
CELERY, finely chopped	1/4 cup			
WALNUTS, chopped	1/4 cup			

SLICED PEACH AND APPLE IN RASPBERRY GELATIN

INGREDIENTS	25 PORTIONS 12- x 12- x 2- in. pan	PORTIONS	PORTIONS	PROCEDURE
RASPBERRY GELATIN	1 cup (6 ounces)			1. Dissolve gelatin in hot water.
BOILING WATER	2 cups			2. Add ice covered with juice and water.
ICE covered with peach juice and water	1-3/4 cups			3. Chill until slightly thickened.
SLICED PEACHES, drained	1 cup			4. Fold in peaches, celery, and apples.
CELERY, finely chopped	1 cup			5. Chill until firm in 12-inch by 12-inch by 2-inch pan.
APPLES, cut in slivers, unpeeled	1 cup			6. Cut in squares (5 x 5). Serve.

INGREDIENTS	PORTIONS	PORTIONS	PORTIONS	PROCEDURE

INGREDIENTS	PORTIONS	PORTIONS	PORTIONS	PROCEDURE

FRUIT SALAD

INGREDIENTS	PORTIONS	PORTIONS	PORTIONS	PROCEDURE

Some fruits and vegetables may be eaten raw. Wedges, leaves, or pieces may take the place of a salad. These should be thoroughly washed. To be palatable, vegetables must be clean and crisp. They may be crisped in the hydrator of an automatic refrigerator or wrapped in a damp clean cloth and placed in the ice box. Fruits with tough skins should be peeled.

FRUIT OR VEGETABLE	25 PORTIONS	NOTES
APPLE OR PEAR WEDGE	1-1/2 pounds	Cut into 1-inch wedges just before serving.
APRICOT HALVES	2 pounds	Cut in halves. Remove stones.
CABBAGE WEDGES	2 pounds	Cut in 1/2-inch wedges. Chop for younger children.
CARROT STICKS	1-1/2 pounds	Select young carrots. Cut into 2-inch lengths and then in thin strips.
CELERY STICKS	1 large bunch	Remove tough strings. Cut into 2-inch pieces.
LETTUCE - HEAD	1 large head	Cut out core. Separate leaves breaking large ones in half.
LETTUCE - LEAF	1-1/2 pounds	Separate leaves and remove ends.
ORANGE OR TANGERINE WEDGES	1-1/2 pounds	Wash and remove skins. Separate into sections.
PEACH WEDGES	2 pounds	Scald peaches, dip in cold water. Peel. Cut in halves, remove stones. Cut in wedges.
SPINACH LEAVES	1 pound	Separate leaves and remove ends.
TOMATO WEDGES	2 pounds	Remove stem. Cut in wedges.
TURNIP STICKS	1-1/2 pounds	Cut into 1/2 inch slices. Pare and cut slices into strips.

CARAMEL APPLES

INGREDIENTS	25 PORTIONS	PORTIONS	PORTIONS	PROCEDURE
CARAMELS	5 lbs.			1. Place caramels in top of double boiler or in trunnion kettle.
WATER	3/4 cup			2. Add water to caramels, heat, stirring frequently, until caramels are melted into smooth sauce.
APPLES* (Eating variety)	25 each medium (140 count)			3. Stick wooden skewers with smooth, flat surfaces into ends of apples which have been washed and dried.
				4. Dip apples into caramel sauce and turn until apple is completely coated.
*Cortland, Delicious, Jonathan, McIntosh, Northern Spy, Roman Beauty, Stayman, Winesap, Wagoner, Wealthy, Winter Banana, Yellow Newtown, York Imperial				5. Place coated apples on wax paper, cool until caramel coating is firm. Place in refrigerator in hot weather or to speed up cooling process.

FROZEN FRUIT SUCKERS

INGREDIENTS	25 PORTIONS 2 ounces	PORTIONS	PORTIONS	PROCEDURE
STRAINED APRICOTS ORANGE JUICE GRANULATED SUGAR You may want to try your own combination of fruit and fruit juice for variety.	1 quart (4 cups) 1 pint (2 cups) 1/4 cup			1. Use canned apricots and blenderize or canned baby food. 2. Combine fruit, juice, and sugar and mix until sugar is dissolved. 3. Pour into firm 3-ounce individual souffle cups. 4. Freeze until mixture is mushy—then insert smooth flat wooden spoons or sturdy smooth plastic spoons. 5. Continue freezing until hard.

INGREDIENTS	PORTIONS	PORTIONS	PORTIONS	PROCEDURE

INGREDIENTS	PORTIONS	PORTIONS	PORTIONS	PROCEDURE

INGREDIENTS	PORTIONS	PORTIONS	PORTIONS	PROCEDURE

Desserts

ROLLED WHEAT-APPLESAUCE COOKIES
or
ROLLED OATMEAL-APPLESAUCE COOKIES

Preheat oven to 375°F.

INGREDIENTS	36 PORTIONS	PORTIONS	PORTIONS	PROCEDURE
APPLESAUCE	1/2 cup			1. Combine applesauce, raisins and rind. Set aside.
RAISINS	1/2 cup			2. In mixing bowl combine sugar, shortening and egg. Beat until light and fluffy.
ORANGE RIND	1 teaspoon			3. Stir in applesauce and raisins.
SUGAR, GRANULATED	1/2 cup			4. Sift dry ingredients together. Add to first mixture. Mix well.
SHORTENING	1/4 cup			5. Stir in rolled wheat or oatmeal and nuts.
EGG	1 each			6. Chill dough.
FLOUR, sifted	1/2 cup			7. Use No. 40 scoop–drop on lightly greased baking sheet.
SALT	1/2 teaspoon			8. Bake 12 to 15 minutes at 375°F.
BAKING POWDER	1/2 teaspoon			
CINNAMON	1/2 teaspoon			
BAKING SODA	1/2 teaspoon			
NUTMEG	1/2 teaspoon			
ROLLED WHEAT	1/2 cup			
OR OATMEAL	1/2 cup			
NUTS, chopped	1/2 cup			

OATMEAL SPICE COOKIES

Preheat oven to 425°F.

INGREDIENTS	36 PORTIONS	PORTIONS	PORTIONS	PROCEDURE
SPICE CAKE MIX	1 package (18-1/2 ounce)			1. In mixer bowl combine cake mix, eggs, oil and water.
EGGS	2 each			2. Stir in oatmeal and raisins until thoroughly mixed.
COOKING OIL	1/2 cup			3. Using No. 40 scoop drop on ungreased cookie sheet.
WATER	1/4 cup			4. Bake at 425°F. for 8 to 10 minutes, until light brown.
OATMEAL	1 cup			
RAISINS	1 cup			

BROWNIES

Preheat oven to 350°F.

INGREDIENTS	36 PORTIONS	PORTIONS	PORTIONS	PROCEDURE
FLOUR, sifted	3 cups			1. Sift flour, baking powder, salt and cocoa together.
BAKING POWDER	1-1/2 teaspoon			2. Add raisins, mix well.
SALT	3/4 teaspoon			3. Mix shortening and sugar until light and fluffy.
COCOA	1 cup			4. Add beaten eggs gradually to shortening and sugar mixture.
RAISINS	1-1/4 cups			5. Add flour mixture, mix only enough to dampen flour.
SHORTENING	1-1/2 cups			6. In 2 well greased 9-inch by 12-inch baking pans spread mixture (about 3/4 inch deep).
SUGAR	3-1/2 cups			7. Bake at 350°F. for 30 minutes.
EGGS, LARGE (well-beaten)	6 each			8. Cut in squares—turn out to cool.
VANILLA	1 tablespoon			

PEANUT BUTTER BARS

Preheat oven to 350°F.

INGREDIENTS	36 PORTIONS	PORTIONS	PORTIONS	PROCEDURE
FLOUR	3 cups			1. Sift flour and baking powder.
BAKING POWDER	1 tablespoon			2. In mixer bowl combine margarine, peanut butter, brown sugar, sugar, salt, eggs and vanilla. Mix on low speed until well blended.
MARGARINE *OR* BUTTER	7 tablespoons			3. Add dry ingredients and mix only until well blended.
PEANUT BUTTER	1-1/2 cups			4. Mix in coconut.
SUGAR	2-1/2 cups + 2 tablespoons			5. Spread mixture in 2 lightly greased 8-inch by 12-inch baking pans.
SALT	3/4 teaspoon			6. Bake at 350°F. for 20 to 25 minutes.
EGGS	6 each			
VANILLA	2 teaspoons			
COCONUT	9 ounces			

NO BAKE OATMEAL CONFECTIONS

INGREDIENTS	PORTIONS 3 dozen	PORTIONS	PORTIONS	PROCEDURE
SUGAR	1 cup			1. Sift sugar, cocoa, milk together.
COCOA	3 tablespoons			2. Place dry ingredients in sauce pan, add water and margarine.
DRIED MILK POWDER	1/2 cup			3. Stir continually and boil for 2 minutes.
MARGARINE *OR* BUTTER	2 tablespoons			4. Add peanut butter and stir until melted.
WATER	1/4 cup			5. Add oatmeal and vanilla and mix completely.
PEANUT BUTTER	1/4 cup			6. Drop by teaspoonsful or No. 40 scoop on wax paper.
OATMEAL (quick cooking)	1-1/2 cups			
VANILLA	1 teaspoon			

PEANUT OAT COOKIES

Preheat oven to 350°F.

INGREDIENTS	25 PORTIONS 2 each	PORTIONS	PORTIONS	PROCEDURE
DRY MILK POWDER	1/3 cup			1. Combine milk powder and water.
WATER *OR*	3/4 cup			2. Combine milk, peanut butter, sugar, oatmeal. Blend thoroughly.
FLUID MILK	(1 cup)			3. On lightly greased cookie sheet, drop by No. 40 scoop.
PEANUT BUTTER	1 pint			4. Bake at 350°F. for 12 to 15 minutes.
SUGAR	1 pint			5. Cool slightly, remove from cookie sheets.
OATMEAL	1 pint			6. Approximately 4 dozen.

CORN MEAL COOKIES

Preheat oven to 400°F.

INGREDIENTS	PORTIONS 6 dozen	PORTIONS	PORTIONS	PROCEDURE
SHORTENING	1 cup			1. Cream shortening, add sugar gradually and cream well.
SUGAR	1 cup			2. Beat in eggs until light and fluffy,
VANILLA	1 teaspoon			3. Add vanilla.
EGGS	2 each			4. Sift flour, corn meal, baking powder. salt, and nutmeg.
ENRICHED FLOUR	3 cups			5. Add flour mixture to creamed mixture, mix thoroughly.
CORN MEAL	1 cup			6. Drop by No. 40 scoop on greased cookie sheet, press with fork and bake in hot oven (400°F.) for 10 minutes–until lightly browned.
BAKING POWDER	1 teaspoon			
SALT	1/2 teaspoon			
NUTMEG	1 teaspoon			

SUPRISE PUFFS

INGREDIENTS	25 PORTIONS	PORTIONS	PORTIONS	PROCEDURE
PUFFED CEREAL	6 cups			1. Place cereal in large greased bowl.
MINIATURE MARSH-MALLOWS	4 cups			2. Melt marshmallows, peanut butter, water, and margarine in top of double boiler or in small trunnion kettle, stirring occasionally until smooth.
PEANUT BUTTER	1/2 cup			3. Pour over cereal, stirring until evenly coated.
WATER	1 tablespoon			4. With greased hands, press into lightly greased 13-inch by 9-inch pan.
MARGARINE *OR* BUTTER	2 tablespoons			5. Let stand 20 minutes.
SEMI-SWEET CHOCOLATE PIECES, melted *OR* BUTTERSCOTCH PIECES, melted	6 oz. package			6. Loosen edges; invert pan to remove cereal mixture.
				7. Cut in half crosswise forming two rectangles.
				8. Spread top of one rectangle with melted chocolate.
				9. Place other rectangle on top of chocolate.
				10. Refrigerate several hours. Cut into bars.

INGREDIENTS	PORTIONS	PORTIONS	PORTIONS	PROCEDURE

INGREDIENTS	PORTIONS	PORTIONS	PORTIONS	PROCEDURE

INGREDIENTS	PORTIONS	PORTIONS	PORTIONS	PROCEDURE

PUMPKIN CAKE

Preheat oven to 350°F.

INGREDIENTS	36 PORTIONS	PORTIONS	PORTIONS	PROCEDURE
SUGAR	4 cups			1. Combine all ingredients EXCEPT FLOUR into mixer. Cream until well blended.
MARGARINE	1-1/2 cups			2. Set mixer, at low speed, slowly add flour.
PUMPKIN	3 cups			3. Continue beating until well mixed.
SALT	1-1/2 teaspoons			4. Grease two 9-inch by 12-inch baking pans.
SODA	1-1/2 teaspoons			5. Divide batter into the two pans. Bake at 350°F. for 40 to 45 minutes. (This is a heavy batter.)
CINNAMON	1-1/2 teaspoons			
ALLSPICE	1-1/2 teaspoons			
VANILLA	1-1/2 teaspoons			
EGGS	4 each			
FLOUR	4-1/2 cups			

INGREDIENTS	PORTIONS	PORTIONS	PORTIONS	PROCEDURE

INGREDIENTS	PORTIONS	PORTIONS	PORTIONS	PROCEDURE

INGREDIENTS	PORTIONS	PORTIONS	PORTIONS	PROCEDURE

ICE CREAM CLOWNS

INGREDIENTS	25 PORTIONS	PORTIONS	PORTIONS	PROCEDURE
COOKIES	25 large round			1. Arrange cookies on sheet pan.
SEEDLESS RAISINS	50 each			2. In center of each cookie place a No. 8 scoop of ice cream.
MARASCHINO CHERRIES	25 each (cut in half)			3. Top ice cream balls with inverted ice cream cone.
ICE CREAM CONES	25 each			Decorate each ball of ice cream with raisin eyes, and cherry nose and mouth.
VANILLA ICE CREAM	1 gallon			
A fun dessert or snack for a special occasion or to celebrate a birthday.				

BUNNY SUNDAES

INGREDIENTS	25 PORTIONS	PORTIONS	PORTIONS	PROCEDURE
ICE CREAM (suggest vanilla or strawberry)	1 gallon			1. On individual plates place a No. 8 scoop of ice cream.
MARSHMALLOW COOKIES	50 each commercial marshmallow cookies			2. Use a cookie for head and tail.
LARGE MARSHMALLOWS	25 cut in half			3. Use marshmallow halves for ears.

Nice to serve at Easter.

INGREDIENTS	PORTIONS	PORTIONS	PORTIONS	PROCEDURE

INGREDIENTS	PORTIONS	PORTIONS	PORTIONS	PROCEDURE

INGREDIENTS	PORTIONS	PORTIONS	PORTIONS	PROCEDURE

FRUIT CRUNCH

Preheat oven to 325°F.

INGREDIENTS	25 PORTIONS	PORTIONS	PORTIONS	PROCEDURE
FRUIT PIE FILLING* CANNED	2 21 ounce cans			1. Grease 10-inch by 14-inch by 2-inch baking pan.
LIGHT BROWN SUGAR, packed	1 cup			2. Spread fruit filling evenly in bottom of pan.
CINNAMON	1 tablespoon			3. Combine sugar, cinnamon and salt.
SALT	1 teaspoon			4. Cut margarine into sugar mixture.
MARGARINE *OR* BUTTER	1/2 cup (soft)			5. Stir in puffed cereal and nuts.
PUFFED WHEAT CEREAL *OR* PUFFED RICE CEREAL	3 cups			6. Sprinkle over top of filling.
WALNUTS *OR* PECANS chopped	1/2 cup			7. Bake at 325°F. for 40 minutes.
*Apricot, Peach, Cherry, Blueberry, Apple, Gooseberry, Raspberry, Strawberry.				8. Portion with No. 20 scoop.

APPLE BETTY

Preheat oven to 350°F.

INGREDIENTS	PORTIONS 1 gallon	PORTIONS	PORTIONS	PROCEDURE
FRESH APPLES, pared, cored and sliced	3 quarts + 1 cup			1. Mix all ingredients together. 2. Place in greased 12-inch by 20-inch by 2-inch pan. 3. Bake at 350°F. for 1 hour or until apples are tender. 4. Portion with No. 10 scoop.
STALE BREAD, cubed	4 cups			
GRANULATED SUGAR	2-1/2 cups			
SALT	3/4 teaspoon			
CINNAMON	1 tablespoon			
RAISINS	2 cups			
MOLASSES	2/3 cup			
LEMON JUICE	2-1/2 tablespoons			
WATER	2/3 quart			
MARGARINE *OR* BUTTER	3/4 cup			

CRANBERRY CRUNCH

Preheat oven to 350°F.

INGREDIENTS	25 PORTIONS	PORTIONS	PORTIONS	PROCEDURE
ROLLED OATS	2 cups			1. Combine dry ingredients and mix thoroughly.
ENRICHED FLOUR	1 cup			2. Add softened margarine and blend until evenly distributed. Mixture will be crumbly.
SALT	1/2 teaspoon			3. Spread half of mixture over bottom of greased 12-inch by 12-inch by 2-inch pan. Pat down. Cover with cranberry sauce–spreading evenly.
LIGHT BROWN SUGAR	2 cups			4. Sprinkle remainder of dry ingredients over cranberries.
MARGARINE, softened	1 cup			5. Bake for 40 minutes in oven at 350° F. Crumbs should be lightly browned. Remove from oven. Let cool before serving. Cut in squares (5 x 5).
CRANBERRY SAUCE, CANNED, whole	2 1 lb. cans			

SCOTCH PUDDING

Preheat oven to 350°F.

INGREDIENTS	25 PORTIONS 2+ ounces	PORTIONS	PORTIONS	PROCEDURE
APPLES, peeled, cored	8 large-cooking			1. Dice apples.
SUGAR	1 cup			2. Combine sugar, cinnamon, and salt.
CINNAMON	1/4 teaspoon			3. In a greased baking pan, place 1/2 of apples.
SALT	1/2 teaspoon			4. Sprinkle with 1/2 of sugar mixture.
MARGARINE	1/4 cup			5. Dot with margarine and place 1/2 of oats over mixture.
OATMEAL	2 cups			6. Repeat steps 3, 4, and 5.
MILK	3 cups			7. Pour milk evenly over top of ingredients.
				8. Cover pan with foil.
				9. Bake at 350°F. for 1 hour.
				0. Remove foil and continue baking for 15 to 20 minutes.
				1. Portion with No. 10 scoop.

TAPIOCA CREAM PUDDING

INGREDIENTS	25 PORTIONS 2 ounces	PORTIONS	PORTIONS	PROCEDURE
EGGS	7 each			1. Separate eggs.
MILK	3 quarts			2. Blend slightly beaten egg yolk with 1 cup milk.
TAPIOCA, INSTANT	1/2 cup			3. Scald remaining milk.
SUGAR	1-1/2 cups			4. Add egg yolk mixture (stirring), tapioca, sugar, and salt to scalded milk.
SALT	1 teaspoon			5. Cook until thickened, stirring continually. Remove from heat.
VANILLA	2 teaspoons			6. Beat egg whites until peaks are formed.
VARIATIONS	*ADD*			7. Fold egg whites into tapioca mixture.
Caramel Tapioca				8. Add vanilla.
Carmelized Sugar	1/2 cup			9. Chill.
Chocolate Tapioca				10. Portion with No. 10 scoop.
Chocolate, melted	1/2 cup			
Fruit Tapioca				
Fold in: drained, diced, canned or fresh fruit or berries	1 quart			

INGREDIENTS	25 PORTIONS 2+ ounces	PORTIONS	PORTIONS	PROCEDURE
SUGAR	1-3/4 cups			1. Combine dry ingredients (sift together).
FLOUR	1/2 cup			2. Blend dry ingredients with 1 pint of cold milk.
CORNSTARCH	1/2 cup			3. Heat remaining 3 quarts of milk to scalding point.
SALT	1 teaspoon			4. Stir in cold milk mixture to hot milk. Cook (stirring) until thickened, about 30 minutes.
MILK	3-1/2 quarts			5. Remove from heat. Add eggs.
EGGS, slightly beaten	9 each			6. Cook 5 to 10 minutes, stirring occasionally.
VANILLA	1 tablespoon			7. Remove from heat, add margarine and vanilla.
MARGARINE, melted	1/4 cup			8. Chill.
				9. Portion with No. 10 scoop.
VARIATIONS	*ADD*			
Caramel				
Carmelized Sugar	1/2 cup			
Chocolate				
Chocolate to hot milk	4 ounces			
Coconut				
Coconut	1-1/2 cups			
Lemon				
Lemon Rind	1 tablespoon			
Lemon Juice	1/2 cup			
Orange				
Orange Rind	1 tablespoon			
Orange Juice	1 cup			

STEAMED FRUIT PUDDING

Preheat oven to 350°F.

INGREDIENTS	25 PORTIONS 2 + ounces	PORTIONS	PORTIONS	PROCEDURE
CAKE or COOKIES, left over	2 pounds or 2 quarts			1. Break cake and cookies into small pieces.
APPLES,* sliced	2-1/2 quarts			2. Turn into greased 9-inch by 15-inch pan.
RAISINS	1/2 cup			3. Cover with apples and raisins.
CINNAMON	1/2 teaspoon			4. Combine cinnamon, brown sugar, margarine, and fruit juice. Heat until sugar is dissolved. Pour over cake-apple mixture.
MARGARINE	1/4 cup			5. Bake in oven at 350°F. or steam for about 1 hour.
FRUIT JUICE	1 pint			6. Portion with No. 10 scoop.
BROWN SUGAR	2-1/2 cups			

*Peaches, Apricots, Cherries, etc. may be used.

RICE CUSTARD

Preheat oven to 350°F.

INGREDIENTS	25 PORTIONS No. 20 scoop	PORTIONS	PORTIONS	PROCEDURE
COOKED RICE	1 quart			1. Thoroughly mix all ingredients.
RAISINS	2 cups			2. Pour into 12-inch by 18-inch buttered baking pan.
SALT	1 teaspoon			3. Bake in water bath for 50 minutes at 350°F.
EGGS, beaten	10 each			4. Portion with No. 20 scoop.
SUGAR, GRANULATED	1-1/2 cups			5. Garnish with whipped topping or piece of fruit.
EVAPORATED MILK *UNDILUTED*	1-1/2 quarts			
WATER	1-1/2 quarts			
VANILLA	1-1/2 tablespoons			
NUTMEG	1 teaspoon			

INGREDIENTS	PORTIONS	PORTIONS	PORTIONS	PROCEDURE

INGREDIENTS	PORTIONS	PORTIONS	PORTIONS	PROCEDURE

INGREDIENTS	PORTIONS	PORTIONS	PORTIONS	PROCEDURE

Breads and Cereals

BREAD DRESSING

Preheat oven to 350°F.

INGREDIENTS	25 PORTIONS No. 20 Scoop	PORTIONS	PORTIONS	PROCEDURE
MARGARINE, melted	1/2 cup			1. Saute celery and onion in margarine until tender. Then set aside to cool.
CELERY, finely chopped	2 cups			2. To fine bread cubes add salt, poultry seasoning, pepper, and parsley, toss lightly together.
ONION, finely chopped	1/4 cup			3. Add sauteed celery and onion and beaten eggs. Mix lightly.
SLICED BREAD, stale, cut in small cubes	2 pounds			4. Place dressing into lightly greased, shallow baking pan.
SALT	1 tablespoon			5. Sprinkle chicken broth and melted margarine over dressing. Bake at 350°F. for 35 to 40 minutes until golden brown.
POULTRY SEASONING	1/2 tablespoon			6. Use No. 20 scoop for serving.
PEPPER	1/2 teaspoon			
PARSLEY, finely chopped	1/2 cup			
EGGS, beaten slightly	2 each			
CHICKEN BROTH	1-1/2 cups			
MARGARINE, melted	1/2 cup			

PEANUT BUTTER FRENCH TOAST

INGREDIENTS	25 PORTIONS	PORTIONS	PORTIONS	PROCEDURE
DRY MILK POWDER	1-1/3 cups			1. Combine milk powder and water.
WATER *OR*	3 cups			2. Gradually beat milk into peanut butter.
FLUID MILK	1 quart			3. Add eggs.
PEANUT BUTTER	1 cup			4. Dip bread into egg and milk mixture.
EGGS	8 each			5. Brush grill with margarine.
BREAD	25 slices			6. Lightly brown bread on one side; turn and brown on other side. Add more margarine if necessary to keep toast from sticking.
MARGARINE	1/4 cup			

CORN MEAL MUSH

INGREDIENTS	25 PORTIONS 1/4 cup	PORTIONS	PORTIONS	PROCEDURE
CORN MEAL	2 cups			1. Mix corn meal, cold water and salt.
COLD WATER	2 cups			2. Slowly stir corn meal mixture into boiling water.
SALT	2 teaspoons			3. Stir and cook until thick.
BOILING WATER	6 cups			4. Lower heat to LOW. Cover and cook 15 minutes, stirring as needed to keep from sticking.
				5. Portion with No. 16 scoop.

FRIED CORN MEAL MUSH

INGREDIENTS	25 PORTIONS 2 oz. slices	PORTIONS	PORTIONS	PROCEDURE
HOT CORN MEAL MUSH FLOUR	See Corn Meal Mush Recipe			1. Put hot corn meal mush into loaf pans. 2. Cool until firm (24 hours). 3. Slice into 2 ounce slices. 4. Dredge mush slices in flour. 5. Fry in heated, greased fry pan or griddle and brown on both sides.

CORN MEAL PANCAKES

INGREDIENTS	25 PORTIONS Small Pancakes	PORTIONS	PORTIONS	PROCEDURE
FLOUR	1 cup			1. Mix flour, corn meal, baking powder, salt, and sugar. Set aside.
CORN MEAL	1 cup			2. Beat eggs in large bowl. Add milk. Add oil.
BAKING POWDER	1 tablespoon + 1 teaspoon			3. Add flour to egg and milk mixture. Stir just enough to mix. (Will be lumpy.)
SALT	1 teaspoon			4. Portion with No. 20 scoop.
SUGAR	2 tablespoons			5. Cook pancakes on heated, greased fry pan or griddle.
EGGS	2 each			6. When pancakes are covered with bubbles, turn and brown other side.
MILK	1-1/2 cups			
COOKING OIL	1/3 cup			

PEANUT BUTTER BREAD

Preheat oven to 350°F.

INGREDIENTS	25 PORTIONS	PORTIONS	PORTIONS	PROCEDURE
FLOUR	2 cups			1. Sift dry ingredients together.
SUGAR	1-1/2 cups			2. Beat eggs, milk, and peanut butter together.
BAKING POWDER	1-1/2 teaspoons			3. Add dry ingredients to egg and milk mixture.
MILK	1 cup			4. Pour in greased 9-inch by 13-inch baking pan.
EGGS	1 each extra large or 2 small			5. Bake for 1 hour. Cool.
PEANUT BUTTER	1 cup			6. Cut in squares.

CORN MEAL GINGERBREAD

Preheat oven to 350°F.

INGREDIENTS	25 PORTIONS	PORTIONS	PORTIONS	PROCEDURE
FLOUR	1 cup			1. Sift flour, corn meal, salt, baking soda and ginger together. Set aside.
CORN MEAL	1 cup			2. Combine margarine, sugar, and egg. Beat well. Stir in molasses.
SALT	1/2 teaspoon			3. Add 1/2 of flour mixture to margarine and sugar. Beat until smooth.
BAKING SODA	1 teaspoon			4. Stir in 1/2 of hot water—add rest of flour mixture and beat until smooth.
GINGER	2 teaspoons			5. Fill greased baking pan 10-inch by 12-inch by 2-inch half full.
MARGARINE *OR* BUTTER	1/2 cup			6. Bake at 350°F. for approximately 45 minutes or until gingerbread springs back.
SUGAR, BROWN	1/2 cup packed			7. Portion (5 x 5) pieces.
EGG	1 each			8. Garnish with whipped topping or applesauce, etc.
MOLASSES	1/2 cup			
HOT WATER	3/4 cup			

INGREDIENTS	PORTIONS	PORTIONS	PORTIONS	PROCEDURE

INGREDIENTS	PORTIONS	PORTIONS	PORTIONS	PROCEDURE

SNACK MIX

Preheat oven to 250°F.

INGREDIENTS	25 PORTIONS 1-1/2 gallon	PORTIONS	PORTIONS	PROCEDURE
MARGARINE	6 tablespoons			1. Melt margarine–add worcestershire sauce, tabasco* sauce, onion salt, and celery salt.
WORCESTERSHIRE SAUCE	1 tablespoon			2. Mix cereals; add sauce and mix lightly.
TABASCO* SAUCE	1/4 teaspoon			3. Bake 2 hours in large roasting pan, stirring every 20 minutes.
ONION SALT	1 teaspoon			4. After cooling, seal in air-tight containers.
CELERY SALT	1 teaspoon			
CHEERIOS*	1 small box			
RICE CHEX*	1 small box			
WHEAT CHEX*	1 small box			
CORN CHEX*	1 small box			
PRETZEL THINS*	1 small box			

**Registered Trade Mark*

CORN MEAL CHEESE CRACKERS

Preheat oven to 400°F.

INGREDIENTS	25 PORTIONS 2 each	PORTIONS	PORTIONS	PROCEDURE
ENRICHED FLOUR, sifted	1-1/4 cups			1. Sift flour, corn meal, and salt together.
CORN MEAL	3/4 cup			2. Cut in shortening until mixture resembles coarse crumbs.
SALT	1 teaspoon			3. Stir cheese into mixture.
SHORTENING	1/2 cup			4. Combine egg and water.
CHEDDAR CHEESE, grated	6 ounces			5. Add egg mixture, 1 tablespoon at a time, to dry mixture–stirring lightly until pastry can be formed into ball.
EGG, beaten	1 each			6. Roll out on lightly floured board to 1/8 inch thickness.
COLD WATER	3 tablespoons			7. With sharp knife, cut strips 1-1/2 inch wide by 3 inches long.
				8. Place on ungreased cookie sheets; prick with fork.
				9. Bake at 400°F. for 8 to 10 minutes.
				10. Cool.

OATMEAL CRACKERS

Preheat oven to 425°F.

INGREDIENTS	25 PORTIONS 2 each	PORTIONS	PORTIONS	PROCEDURE
ENRICHED FLOUR, sifted	3/4 cup			1. Sift flour and salt together.
SALT	3/4 teaspoon			2. Cut in shortening until mixture resembles fine crumbs.
SHORTENING	1/4 cup			3. Stir in cheese and oatmeal.
CHEDDAR CHEESE, grated	3 ounces			4. Sprinkle water by tablespoon over mixture—stirring with fork after each addition.
OATMEAL, QUICK COOKING	3/4 cup			5. Form into ball; flatten and shape into a square.
COLD WATER	6 tablespoons			6. Roll out on lightly floured board to 1/8-inch thick.
PAPRIKA				7. With sharp knife, cut into 2-inch squares.
				8. Place on ungreased cookie sheet—1 inch apart.
				9. Bake at 425°F. for 12 to 15 minutes—until browned. Sprinkle with paprika. Crackers should be crisp.

INGREDIENTS	PORTIONS	PORTIONS	PORTIONS	PROCEDURE

INGREDIENTS	PORTIONS	PORTIONS	PORTIONS	PROCEDURE

Miscellaneous

SALAD DRESSINGS

MAYONNAISE

INGREDIENTS	PORTIONS 1 quart	PORTIONS	PORTIONS	PROCEDURE
EGG YOLKS SALT PEPPER, WHITE MUSTARD, DRY SUGAR SALAD OIL VINEGAR, CIDER (50 grain)	3 large 1-3/4 teaspoons Dash 1-1/2 teaspoons 2 teaspoons 3 cups 5 tablespoons			1. Beat egg yolks on high speed until light and thick, approximately 5 minutes. 2. Mix salt, pepper, mustard and sugar together. 3. Add dry ingredients to egg yolks and continue mixing on high speed for 3 minutes. 4. Add a little of the oil—then a little vinegar, blending at high speed for about 7 minutes. The oil should be incorporated well each time before vinegar is added. Finish up with vinegar. *NOTE:* Too rapid addition of oil may cause mayonnaise to separate. If the slightest separation occurs around the edge of the bowl, stop adding oil and add vinegar.

CLEAR FRENCH DRESSING

INGREDIENTS	PORTIONS 1 quart	PORTIONS	PORTIONS	PROCEDURE
CIDER VINEGAR (50 grain)	1-1/3 cups			1. Mix all ingredients thoroughly. (Blender or shaker jar may be used.) 2. Mix ingredients again each time before using.
SALAD OIL	2-2/3 cups			
WORCESTERSHIRE SAUCE	1/4 teaspoon			
DRY MUSTARD	1 teaspoon			
SALT	3 tablespoons			
PEPPER	Dash			
SUGAR	1 tablespoon			

COTTAGE CHEESE DRESSING

INGREDIENTS	25 PORTIONS No. 20 Scoop	PORTIONS	PORTIONS	PROCEDURE
CREAM COTTAGE CHEESE	2 pounds			1. Mix ingredients in order given. (Either blender or mixer can be used.)
SALAD DRESSING	1/4 cup			2. Mixture should be soft and not stiff. If it is stiff enough to hold its shape, thin mixture with milk to desired consistency.
ONION, grated	1 tablespoon			
SALT	1/2 tablespoon			

Index

ABOUT THE AUTHOR

Patricia D. Asmussen, R. D., is presently Nutrition Consultant in the Division of Hospital and Institutional Services, Indiana State Board of Health, Indianapolis.

Her articles on nutrition and young children have appeared in *Nutrition and Feeding of Infants and Children Under Three in Group Day Care*, published by HEW, and the *Indiana State Board of Health Bulletin.* She also writes the "Food-Fun 'N Facts" column for *Day In Care,* published four times yearly by the Indiana State Department of Public Welfare.

Mrs. Asmussen, who holds an M. S. in Dietetic Education, is treasurer of the Indiana Nutrition Council and a member of the American Dietetic Association and the Indiana Coordinate Community Child Care Committee.